profits and cash! Something which the very great majority of vets do not properly understand and their financial wellbeing suffers significantly because of it.

As Diederik can testify, because he has now taught his concepts to many, small changes to the way a vet operates his or her practice can generate massively positive improvements in sales, profits and cash.

It's time our Australian vets generated the kind of financial security which many other professionals experience as well as a comfortable lifestyle and an assured, stress-free retirement.

Diederik's book and the concepts it contains will most assuredly be the road map for this outcome.

Damien Parker
Small Business Management Consultant | Increasing SALES, PROFITS & CASH better, faster, smarter!
www.salesprofitscash.com
Queensland, Australia

I0111556

Testimonial – Dr Paolo Lencioni

When my wife and I moved to Australia from the UK and decided to switch from being veterinarians to accountants, Diederik was one of the few people who had the vision to see the true potential of what we were going to do.

It was at one of his coaching groups and along with some of the mentors that attended that we made the decision to only service only the veterinary industry and nobody else as an accounting firm. This was one of the best business decisions we ever made, and Diederik was instrumental in helping us make it.

Over the years that followed we have seen Diederik continue to make a difference in the veterinary industry by making the profession more aware of the importance of running an efficient business so that work life balance is possible.

Paolo Lencioni, BVSc DipCAP MPA
APL Accountants & CloudSwirl Pty Ltd (Bee Free Software | Slyncy)
Cleveland, Queensland

Testimonial – Dr Peter Weinstein

The practice of veterinary medicine and the conduct of veterinary business on the surface looks very complex. There are lots of moving parts that bring with them tremendous potential for failure. HOWEVER, there are many practices that have been able to figure what works. Whatever it is that they do is not 'rocket science', they have just figured out the secrets.

Success leaves clues and those practices that have it figured out are a great resource for others to learn from, emulate, and then become successful on their own. By interviewing and writing the story of successful veterinarians, Dr Gelderman has provided a treasure trove of tips, tricks, thoughts, and ideas that any practice can use…and they been tested and proven already!!

All too often veterinarians try to do everything by themselves refusing to seek outside help. However, there is a huge tendency for veterinarians to follow what others have done successfully. Diederik has gathered in one source what your colleagues have done to reach the top. Learn from the best how to be the best.

Dr Diederik Gelderman has a passion to help the veterinary profession move forward to greater success in practice and to move veterinarians forward to greater success in life. Take this opportunity to move both your practice and yourself forward by learning how others have done so.

Peter Weinstein, DVM, MBA
PAW Consulting & Southern Californian Veterinary Medical Association
California

Testimonial – Christine Tsaloumas

Diederik offers insight from his own experiences and years of helping peers achieve great outcomes, he helps you set goals that you can reach.

It is rare to have someone inspire you over and over, offering new and insightful ways to bring out the best in you.

Diederik has a way of stimulating your mind, filling it with knowledge and setting it alight with ideas to not only motivate you but also to bring out the best in your business and challenge yourself.

Diederik continues to deliver and integrate ways to grow your business. He leaves a lasting impression and once you start on his journey he leaves you wanting more.

Chris Tsaloumas
(Cenvet Victoria)

Praise For The Author

Testimonial – Chris Newton

Do you know that feeling when you meet a fellow vet, and you get to learn about their experiences in running a practice?

Perhaps in that encounter, they let you in on how they manage to balance lifestyle, family and career, while running a busy, happy, growing practice. Or they share some simple but brilliant strategies they discovered to get their team more focused, energised and motivated. Or how they've overcome the very challenges you've been struggling with, to deal with price-cutting vets down the road.

Whatever revelations you may glean in those precious moments with a switched-on fellow vet, I think you'll agree it can leave you invigorated, re-motivated, and absolutely buzzing with new ideas. Ideas you know you can take away and implement in your own practice.

Well, multiply that buzz! Multiply it by about 20 or 30 times…

That is the feeling you'll get as you read *Veterinary Practice Success Secrets Revealed*! By writing this book, Diederik Gelderman has given you a wonderful gift.

Diederik, as you probably know, makes it his life purpose to be constantly rubbing shoulders with practice owners. Coaching them yes, but learning from them too. After decades at the front line with veterinarians the world over, he knows all the success secrets.

In *Veterinary Practice Success Secrets Revealed*, he has captured a treasure trove of wisdom and practical advice from a 'mastermind' of REALLY successful vets. His masterstroke was to capture THEIR words, and to and edit them into a series of searching, in-depth, power-packed interviews.

I cannot commend this book enough to you. It is indeed, an absolute treasure trove of ideas, inspiration, practical tips and strategies for you as a busy, time pressed practice owner. You won't be able to read this without profiting from it in many ways.

I congratulate Diederik for this initiative. I just wish I had thought of it first!

Chris Newton
Co-founder, Ultimate Veterinary Practice Program and Director Results Interactive Training
The Gap, Queensland

Testimonial – Damien Parker

When Diederik Gelderman ran his book concept past me I immediately said *"Diederik, there is nobody better qualified to write this book than yourself. After all, you've seen this industry from every angle and unlike most writers, you've actually been in the trenches and experienced the day to day issues and frustrations. You know intimately how this industry ticks."*

I truly believe that because I have known and observed Diederik and his business methodologies for over 20 years. I was in awe of the customer service standards of his vet practice at Maitland – truly cutting edge and I took his examples to the Australian small business community via my widely-circulated newsletter – 'Positive Business' – for one very strong reason, they worked!

I then had the privilege of helping him implement a number of successful marketing strategies into his vet practice to build the average dollar spend and improve the recurrence of regular services– something quite rare back then. He certainly ran with the concept and created appropriate systems to cater for this.

Then, around ten years ago Diederik pioneered a brilliant coaching/ consulting model for the veterinarian fraternity which focused on a concept near and dear to my heart. The absolute importance of sales,

VETERINARY
SUCCESS
Secrets Revealed

GLOBAL
PUBLISHING
G R O U P

Global Publishing Group
Australia • New Zealand • Singapore • America • London

VETERINARY SUCCESS

Secrets Revealed

How To Have An Amazing Practice And Achieve Work-Life Balance

REE PRACTICE BUILDING TOOLS INSIDE

Dr Diederik Gelderman

First Edition 2017

National Library of Australia

Cataloguing-in-Publication entry:

Creator: Gelderman, Diederik, author.

Title: Veterinary Success Secrets Revealed: How to Have an Amazing Practice and Achieve Work-Life Balance / Dr Diederik Gelderman.

ISBN: 9781925288582 (paperback)

Subjects: Success in business.
Veterinary hospitals.
Work-life balance.
Veterinarians.

Published by Global Publishing Group
PO Box 517 Mt Evelyn, Victoria 3796 Australia
Email info@GlobalPublishingGroup.com.au

For further information about orders:
Phone: +61 3 9739 4686 or Fax +61 3 8648 6871

This book is dedicated to all the boys and girls and young men and women all over the world who dared to dream of one day helping animals and people through the art and science of being a veterinarian.

Follow your heart and dream, stay focused and on track, look at the bigger picture and keep at it.

Resilience, sticking-to-it-ness as well as your dedication will make it all come true for you.

Use these inspiring stories, of how others achieved their dreams and learn how you can do it too…

Acknowledgements

It's been an honour and a privilege to be able to write this book. Without the help and support of a number of very special people, it would never have made the light of day and therefore I'd like to take this opportunity to stay a very big 'Thank You' to those responsible.

Although it is my name that appears on the cover, ultimately this book has a multitude of authors.

I would firstly like to thank the contributors who followed their dreams and their passions – without you, there would simply have been no 'special story' and no book. For your struggle and perseverance, I would like to congratulate and thank you. I also appreciate your time which you have so freely given me and your trust in allowing me to share your success journey. For this and everything else…I am incredibly grateful.

Next, I need to thank my many mentors, models, guides, colleagues and friends who have been with me supporting, inspiring, motivating me and even kicking my butt when it was necessary.

These people have all been incredible gifts in my life, gifts which in many cases, at the time did not appear as such.

Most importantly to start with are my coaches, including Damien Parker and Patrick Lumbroso. Without you two and your belief in me, none of this would have been possible.

And then my two great friends and personal trainers Adrian Brough and Carmen Jeffrey. Without you two helping me to keep my body in shape, my mind would never have survived.

I've been studying personal development since I was 17 and without Nightingale Conant, I would never have been able to even start on this success path – for that I owe them a huge vote of thanks.

Next I need to acknowledge my personal growth mentors. These include;

the Buddha, H.H. the Dalai Lama, Tony Robbins, Christopher Howard, Brian Tracy, Pat Mesiti and Jim Rohn.

My business skills, marketing acumen and general savvy have come about thanks to Frank Kern, Brendon Burchard, Darren Hardy, Jay Abraham, Chris Newton, Thomas Catanzaro (Tom Cat), Michael Gerber, Peter Weinstein, John Sheridan and Paul Dunn.

Then there are my family and friends, people who believed in me and supported me, even when I was personally lost and could not see the possibilities that they could.

They include Brian Pickering, Kaye Brown, Judy Gillespie, Christine Moxon, Craig Toyne, Michelle Brough, Kim Kendall. Michele Elmas and Valerie Cooper.

Of course, this list of acknowledgements would not be complete without mentioning my special family. Mum, thanks for always being there; Dad – wish you'd been around longer; Herold and Anita, I look up to you and what you've achieved both in your business and with your devoted family every day – you're a rock in my life. And then of course Jody, Karinne and Dane – you guys are awesome.

When mentioning family, there is my overseas family, family who I wish were much closer and I see them far too infrequently. Uncle Henk, I miss you. You taught me so much in the little time we had together. Then there is Bep, Ben, Jody, Henk, Belinda and the rest of the family. You know who you are so I won't list you all here. And then of course the 'Spanish' connection – Sette and Nathalie.

I'd also like to thank all the wonderful people that I worked with on the AVPMA which subsequently became the AVBA. You guys were a true gift in my life, just when I needed it.

There's a very important person, without whom NONE of this would have been possible, my partner Jennifer. I owe you a huge debt of thanks and love for the support, guidance and love that you give me, and your belief in me!

These acknowledgements would not be complete without a very special mention of my former wife Talia Grushka and my former business partner Lionel Bloom.

My one-on-one students, I thank you as well for all the learnings that you have shared with me. I always learn as much from you as you from me.

Lastly and most importantly of all, two people who have been lighthouses in my storms – and I've had numerous storms – I need to thank Paul Lloyd and Mark Simm. Mark, my best friend ever, who died far, far too young, I miss you every day. And Paul, I've tried hard to see life through your really 'different' eyes, please keep letting me see.

Ultimately, with all the great support that I've had, there is no doubt that I've missed acknowledging someone. If that's the case, you know who you are and I thank you sincerely for everything that you've done.

Diederik Gelderman

FREE RESOURCES
Valued at $3,995

I can't give you everything you need to know about how to have an amazing practice and achieve work-life balance in one small book (even though this book is a GREAT starting point).

So, I've created lots of extra special goodies just for you. These include:

- Training programs to fast track your success.

- Advanced concepts, business insights and marketing leverage ideas to help you realise the vision you have for your veterinary business.

- Resources to help you get your personal life back on track and achieve the level of personal and professional satisfaction that you so rightly deserve.

- Membership to the Veterinary Business Academy – a community of like-minded individuals.

- Transcribed interviews and audio files.

Go to
www.VeterinarySuccessSecretsRevealed.com
to get instant access and **FREE** tools to create your own
'Success Journey'.

Contents

Foreword

Dr Mark O'Byrne
BSc(Hons) BVetMed MRCVS
Veterinary Affairs Manager
Hill's Pet Nutrition

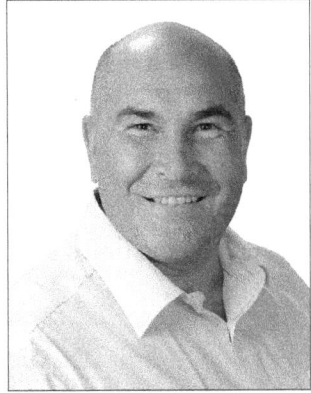

My first encounter with an Australian vet was in my first year as a young graduate in mixed rural practice, at that most impressionable time in one's career. To have someone on your shoulder with a few years of wisdom under their belt and clearly enjoying life to the full made my first couple of years so much easier – and more importantly, fun. That opened my mind to the possibility of learning through mistakes and the concept of leaving my comfort zone by putting my career in a backpack and exploring the world out there.

To be invited to be part of this book as a "Pom" surprised me pleasantly, but the real words that sprang to mind were 'honour' and 'privilege', to be counted alongside colleagues who have led the way for the rest of us and for those to follow.

I met many Antipodean vets and nurses in the 90s, pioneering veterinary medicine and surgery throughout Asia at a time when pet ownership was burgeoning and the standards of care were improving exponentially. Many of those veterinarians remain there and continue their quests to bring modern veterinary care and standards to those parts of the world that need it most.

When I finally arrived in Australia, with a remit to build relationships with the veterinary profession in both Australia and New Zealand, I was warmly welcomed by new colleagues and friends. Lively characters full of zest and a keen interest in the success of others were abound, always willing to support their peers and where differences existed, common ground was found. This made my task relatively easy, especially as we all have common goals – to serve the patients we advocate for, to provide the care that they need and deserve and to make our world a better place by employing the finest veterinary and communication skills.

Our profession has changed a lot in the last 20 years, we face many challenges and paradigm shifts and some of our colleagues have had to overcome great adversity. I have always found 'The Desiderata' a great resource when times are tough:

'Take kindly to the counsel of the years, gracefully surrendering the things of youth. Nurture strength of spirit to shield you in sudden misfortune. But do not distress yourself with dark imaginings. Many fears are born of fatigue and loneliness.'

There are many reasons to pick up and share this book, no matter how far along your career journey you are. The secrets that are revealed by the veterinarians in this book are insightful, wise, simple and actionable by anyone. That is, in my opinion, the real power that's revealed here. Everyone can implement these strategies and achieve happiness and success. I urge you to read this book from cover to cover and then take action on what you learn. Collectively, I'm sure that the stories and accounts of our careers will help yours in one way or another. Don't be tired or lonely, strive to be happy.

I have nothing but admiration for Diederik and this much-needed record of the contribution we all make to our profession. My final words are "humbled" and "proud". The individuals in this book are just the tip of an iceberg that is known as the Great Australian Veterinary Profession.

Introduction

Thank you so very much for investing in and making time to read this book. Let me share with you:

- WHY I wrote it
- WHO it is for
- HOW to use it
- And WHAT your next step is

Over the last 15-plus years that I have been coaching and mentoring veterinary practice owners all over the world. There's been a common theme, a common thread from those I have talked to and it goes something like this: *"I've seen those successful vets in journals, at events and showcased here, there and everywhere, but I don't have what they have, they're special, I don't have their skills, their talents, I've tried, but I just can't get it to work…"*

You know what – you DO have what they have, they're NOT so special or gifted or unique that you can't be too!

One of my biggest purposes in writing this book is to help eliminate that excuse that I hear so many vets make of: *"I'm not special like those 'successful' vets."*

And I've done that by interviewing a large group of 'Average-Joe' type practitioners, practitioners who are not industry icons nor household names – and yet who are very successful indeed.

Let me explain…

As well as those 'iconic' vets that we've all heard of, there's a much larger group of so-called 'ordinary vets' (of whom you've NEVER heard), who also have successful, amazing careers and awesome lives.

These 'ordinary practitioners' don't have any 'magic formula' or 'secret to success' – no more than you have. They're not more talented, gifted or luckier than you either. Most of them have followed a very simple path to success.

Once you've seen what they've done, once you've seen that path and how they followed it, you can do it too.

Do what they did and 'success' will inevitably be yours as well.

I want to make it easy for you to follow that same path and therefore to make it easy for you to achieve that success, I've interviewed a range of successful practitioners from all over Australia.

Most interviews in this book are of these 'average' vets whom you may never have heard of but who are, successful in every definition of that word and who have built a worthwhile life, balancing work, career, family and lifestyle in their 'average' (to you but not to their clients) practices.

I want to share how you too can achieve what they have. I want you to understand that it's not rocket science, doesn't involve genius, you don't need the best 'toys' or a multi-million-dollar facility and how by applying basic, common sense principles, staying true to your path and following your dream you can achieve it too.

And then in contrast to successful practitioners who are largely unheralded, I've also interviewed the well-recognised, well-known, public veterinary icons with household names. I've included this group very deliberately to show you various alternate and alternative career paths that you could choose to go down, should that be your interest.

When you read the stories of the 'TV Vet' or the 'Cat Vet', the 'Alternative Medicine Vet' or the 'Corporate Vet' etc., you could easily ask me *"Why didn't you interview Dr XXX or Dr YYY?"*

The answer is simply that there were far too many inspiring stories around and I could not interview 'everyone'. I chose those who I thought gave the best overall perspective to you, the reader, and gave you the most insight as to how you can also do what they did.

Those other great vets – I'm sure they will make for a very good second book ☺.

In summary:

There are many ways to be successful and to have a worthwhile life – I know that reading these inspiring stories will make your journey, your path, easier.

These stories will act as an inspiration and as a guide for you, so that when you become lost or stray from the path you can follow their example, take their lead say: *"I can do this too…"* or *"This is what I need to do next….!"*

Your next step: 'DO SOMETHING!' This book itself is simply your starting point. Here is what to do next.

Firstly: This book contains only some of the interviews that I did in the making of this book. There were far too many wonderful stories to fit into 400 pages and so I've uploaded EVERYTHING to the www.VeterinarySuccessSecretsRevealed.com website where you can access them with my compliments.

Secondly: Most of the vets that I interviewed were SO generous with their time that the interviews went well over what could be included here (without creating a 1000-page edition)! In the chapters, you see the 'best of the best' snippets of the interviews. In fact, most of the interviews had to be condensed by 50% or even more –

There was an AMAZING amount of very valuable information that simply could not be included. Therefore, you can get access to the FULL INTERVIEWS at the www.VeterinarySuccessSecretsRevealed.com

Thirdly: Go to the Recommended Resources page to access a host of free resources. There are a huge number of tips, tools, templates and strategies that you can use, implement and apply immediately. All you need to do is to personalise them and mould them to suit your preferences.

As I said earlier, it's not rocket science, it's not hard, you can do it too, you just need to put your mind to it.

ACT now and start to achieve the level of personal and professional satisfaction, that inspiring and happy life that you deserve. Do that and in the next book I will be interviewing YOU.

How To Use This Book For Maximum Impact

Over the last 15 years, working as a business coach/mentor to veterinarians from all over the world, I've seen the extremes of non-achievement through to great success.

In all cases of non-achievement through to all cases of success there are similar and obvious underlying patterns and themes.

The purpose of this book is to interview a broad range of the 'successful' veterinarians and document the common 'drivers' to success, so that any veterinarian who is 'stuck', not achieving what they'd like to, who is unsure of what path, direction to take or what that next step should be, can find a 'role-model' in these pages and using those exact same success drivers, become successful in his or her own right.

They can find someone with a similar story, and see what that person did, how they did it and then find a way forward in their own career by implementing some of the strategies that have lead others to success.

That's why I've interviewed veterinarians with all sorts of different journeys and ended up with many different practices, practice types and career paths.

Everyone I've interviewed has one trait in common – that is that they are 'successful'.

They are successful in and to themselves. This does not mean that they are recognised by the public at large or that they are TV personalities (even though in fact some of these veterinarians are widely recognised and are TV personalities).

Most the interviews in this book consist of 'average' vets, vets whom you may never have heard of but who are 'successful and have built a worthwhile life, balancing work, family and lifestyle in their 'average' (to you, but not to their clients) practices.

I want to share how you can achieve those levels of success for yourself and how you don't have to be a rocket scientist, have a genius level IQ or be a master marketer to achieve all that. You don't even have to be a specialist, have the best building or all the latest 'toys'....

In fact, I want you to appreciate how one can in fact be 'ordinary' (if that's the right term) and still be eminently successful and have an inspiring and a happy life.

Most certainly the well-recognised and very public vets are also showcased in this book. I have included interviews with well-known, public veterinary icons, those with household names.

I've included this wide range of veterinarians to show you a gamut of alternative and/or different career paths that you could choose to go down, all of which can lead you to your 'success'.

I can't stress enough, that I'm sharing these varied stories of what different vets have done and how they've done it, so that you can see how easy it is, how simple it is and how you can do it too.

Let these people act as an inspiration and a guide to you, so that when you are 'lost' you can take out their example, hold it up and say – *"Hey, I can do this too."*

There are many ways to be successful and to have a worthwhile life – I'm hoping that reading these stories will make your journey to success easier.

Success is simple and is just a matter of:
- applying some basic, common-sense principles
- following some simple, tried and true strategies
- and following your dream whilst staying true to yourself and to your dream

How To Use This Book

There are hundreds of successful veterinarians that I could have showcased in this book, but then you would have to spend all your time reading rather than taking action on what you learn!

I chose those whom I think are the best of the best and I recorded those interviews for you either live or via Skype.

Since everyone was so generous with their time, the interviews were all far too in-depth and far too long to be fully included in this book. As it was, to fit them in, I had to reduce them by 50% to 60%.

So you won't miss out on anything, I've ensured that you can get access to the full, unabridged interviews with my compliments by going to www.VeterinarySuccessSecretsRevealed.com

Go there to access;

- the **full video**
- the **full transcript** and
- the **entire audio recordings** of every interview.

While you are there, you can also access the **BONUS interviews** that I did for you and which could not be contained in this book.

Complementary Resources

To give you an unfair advantage on your journey to success, I've personally hand-picked some awesome, bonus resources for you. You will find them in the back of this book and you'll also find them on the www.VeterinarySuccessSecretsRevealed.com website. Make sure you check them out.

Using these tools, templates, strategies and resources will turbo-charge your ability to make your practice successful, maybe even more successful than the veterinarians I've interviewed in this book.

These resources are there for you with my compliments – please make use of them. You've got no excuses if you don't!

Dr Ari Ende

Dr Ari Ende

BSC (Zoology), BVSc (Honours)

> *"The better I get to know men, the more I find myself loving dogs."* ~ Charles de Gaulle

Ari Ende is a Sydney-based mobile vet, passionate about quality veterinary care and specifically about helping to maintain the close bond and companionship between his clients and their pets. Ari has 17 years' experience in small animal medicine and surgery and is a member of the Australian and New Zealand College of Veterinary Scientists in Small Animal Medicine.

On graduation in 2000, Ari immediately moved to the country and worked in mixed animal practice, where he spent a year and half.

Upon coming back to Sydney, he spent several years working as a clinical registrar at the University Veterinary Teaching Hospital Sydney. Following this he worked in a few small animal practices in Sydney, including a year and a half of emergency and critical care work, before starting his own mobile veterinary service VET Around Sydney Mobile Vet Service.

Ari has run this business for the last eight years continuing to grow in this high-demand niche area. The decision to become a 'house call vet' was a no-brainer (at least his wife thought so) when Ari realised what a great service he could offer owners and their pets by attending to them in their own homes, while maintaining a 'best practice' veterinary medicine approach. His goal was to offer a home consultation service without compromising the quality of veterinary care that clients expected for their pets.

Ari with his wife Nicky, have a young family; two girls, and a little boy. They share their lives with two boisterous dogs, and three more independent and very loved cats. Ari's family is rather 'full' but he wouldn't have it any other way.

DIEDERIK: Ari, what ignited your passion to become a vet, and at what age did you make that decision?

ARI: When I graduated from school, I enrolled in electrical engineering. I left engineering after four weeks realising it wasn't my passion. I took a year off and did a lot of soul searching. The health industry because I liked the medical side of things was obvious, and I was passionate about animals. It came together then that I wanted to be a vet. I was basically a professional student for the 90s, and graduated in 2000 a vet.

DIEDERIK: So, looking back now, what didn't they teach you at Uni that you know now is crucial to being a successful vet?

ARI: When we graduated, we graduated as technicians essentially. We're trained to be medical technicians. And, the ability to function in the real world when you leave University and put your medical knowledge into real practice in real people's lives, that's not great.

What you must learn is how to make that medical knowledge work for your clients and for your patients. Handling animals, handling people's emotions. Communicating to someone in a consultation, and making those people feel like they've been heard and getting a good service for that pet. There's a lot of emotions running high, and it's one of the scariest things, to be thrust into a consult room on your own. Suddenly you've got to apply all this knowledge and really, you don't know what you're doing.

So, the technical side of things are there, and you have to just learn how to make that work in practice. But, the other side of stuff about working within a business, working with people's emotion, communicating, that's tough to teach, and that's probably one of the scariest things.

? DIEDERIK: The other side of the coin, what did they teach you at vet school that now you know is not true?

ARI: At university – you learn in a referral setting and you learn medical practice of the highest standard. Then you get into the real world then suddenly, you've got people that can't afford 'the best'. You've got tests and diagnostic pathways that aren't so available, and suddenly you actually have got to rejig how you offer your medical service because you can't offer everything.

? DIEDERIK: What are three things that a new graduate needs to do as soon as possible to turbocharge their career?

ARI: You need to put some effort into that and make a plan.

First, it will help you get an idea of where do you want to start. Once you've got that in place, let's say you want to get into private practice, or maybe you want to do a bit of zoo work, or maybe you want to do something completely different. But, if you're going to go into clinical practice, you want to make sure you go into the most supportive practice you can. Don't be afraid to interview the practice. They're interviewing you to seal your place, you interview them back. It will make sure that it's where you think you're going to get the best support.

The worst experience for most new grads that get into a practice, is they're on their own, and they are struggling. So, that's (one) plan, (two) serious support, genuine support.

? DIEDERIK: The other side of that coin, what are two or three things that a new graduate has to avoid doing, to turbo-charge their career?

ARI: Avoid being arrogant. Avoid thinking that you must know everything. We want people to think we know what we're doing.

Don't be afraid to show that you don't necessarily know what you're doing, which is hard for a 21- or 22-year-old to do; it's easier for a 30-year-old to do, and even easier for me now as a 47-year-old to do, and I think honesty is always the best policy. Don't be that arrogant new graduate that thinks that they can do anything.

Don't rush into taking the first job that's offered to you, unless you know that it's right. Go and put yourself out there, have a few interviews. Feel like you're just looking around with care.

DIEDERIK: Thank you. So, if you were starting again, would you in fact be a vet?

ARI: I really don't know. But at the moment, no. For me now, I probably would have done medicine. That sounds odd, and I think I'm probably a better vet than I'd be as a doctor, maybe. I mean I do love working with pets, and I love every day. So often, I just think how lucky am I to be a vet. But, financially, it's very tough.

DIEDERIK: What were three major challenges that you faced in getting to where you are?

ARI: I was probably my biggest challenge. I grew up with a pretty easy life. I didn't really have to look after myself, and I didn't know what I wanted to do, and then it was hard for me to figure that out. I turned out to be a vet, but that felt really good. None of my friends thought I'd get a job because they all thought I'd be a student for the rest of my life. And God, getting work after the University, I can't imagine it being that, which I did immediately, and I haven't looked back, but it might be because of my own fear, and I'm still challenged by that, absolutely. Even right now Diederik, I mean this is a very timely interview, to be frank. You heard good feedback about me in the industry, which is fantastic, which definitely helps. And my confidence is definitely higher than it ever has been over all, just in my ability to provide the service that I'm providing. But I still have my fear every day, and I'm still at a bit of a crossroads now, trying to work out what I want to do with my business. So, that's a big one. Learn about yourself as well as you can, and try to work out how to work with your own emotions as best as you can.

The biggest challenge at the moment is managing my work and family balance. How to be a dad and a husband, and how to be a businessman, and how to be vet all at the same time.

DIEDERIK: What does success look like to you?

ARI: Success has many facets. People commonly look at financial success, and I'd like to have financial success. I don't think I'm there yet, but we're doing okay. My personal success with my chosen career, and that's about how I feel as a vet. And right now, I can see that what I've put in place has hit the mark. And a measurement of my success is also my confidence and my ability to do that. So, that's a more internal emotion on what success is, which I think is extremely important.

My biggest success is that I've got something that I built up. And the feedback, it's more positive than it is negative, and that's a big story.

Then, success, in terms of owning a business, because not every vet runs a business, most are employees. Running a successful business would be the point where you can step out of your business and be able to work in it in the way you want to without it falling apart without you, and I'm not there yet.

DIEDERIK: What do you think have been the keys to your current achievements?

ARI: Firstly, the ability to tolerate tough times. Everyone talks about overnight success. But everyone has a little tough time to their own success story. People very easily don't tolerate tough feelings; tolerate the time it takes once you put a plan in place to make it happen.

And then, it's important to be able to have the right people around you. That doesn't relate to any specific area of business, just whatever you think you need for your career path, to be able to turn to for advice, or turn to for a shoulder to lean on. Having the people around you that are supportive. It's easy for some people just to get the mindset of having to do it all on his own...the longer I work, the longer I realise that that's certainly not true.

And, work to your strengths. My strength is my relationship building. My key strength would be being able to communicate with people.

And to have the right empathy for my patients, and people.

DIEDERIK: So, what have you found are the best methods for you to keep you motivated and focused?

ARI: Firstly, outside of the vet industry, and outside of business, one of the biggest thing to keep yourself motivated, is an outlet for you yourself. For me, it's physical outdoor activity. Whatever it is for you, do it so that you're not a grumpy man for the rest of the day.

Another motivation would be just the knowledge that I've got a beautiful family, and I need to just keep doing what I'm doing for them.

Then another key motivation comes from work itself. I've chosen to be a vet, my work is providing health care, but when you can see the impact that your job has on so many, sometimes that's all it takes for you to keep going because on some days, you don't feel like you're doing any good at all, and you realise you got to keep going.

DIEDERIK: You said earlier that if you were doing it again, you may not be a vet, but if you were being a vet, and you had the chance to do it all again, what would you do differently if anything?

ARI: The only reason I said that I probably wouldn't be a vet, is that I'm not a businessman; and financially, it's a struggle. So, that's the only reason I said I'd be a doctor, but to be honest, I'd probably would be a vet again.

I probably wouldn't do that much differently in terms of the steps that happened.

But what I'd possibly do differently is just continually being aware of myself. I said one of the biggest challenges for me was me, my own fear, and I'd probably just not be as hard on myself. And that's one thing that I'm learning, to listen to things around you. Listen to what's going on in your body, don't ignore them, and don't feel like you must prove a point to anyone, or prove that you're the best. I'd probably do that a bit differently if had the ability to do so, and be a bit more mindful of that kind of thing.

DIEDERIK: What do you think stops most vets from achieving their goals?

ARI: I think one of the biggest things that holds us back is our lack of self-confidence in our own ability – not ability, that's not the right word – in our own position in the work place, in society in general.

Just our sense of self-respect and not being bullied into doing something that either we're not capable of doing or don't want to do if you don't feel it's okay.

DIEDERIK: Do you think that tragedy or luck has played a part in achieving your success?

ARI: Luck, yes, absolutely. I mean, being with the right people at the right place at the right time getting that job is the answer about the universe providing it. Obviously, you also need to be putting yourself in that place at the time, and if you didn't do that, you wouldn't be there.

Tragedy. I come from a very traditional Jewish family, and I probably have to say tragedy probably has shaped my life. And in terms of my overall mental health and just perceptions of the world, my own capacity as a human being, that's been largely shaped by tragedy, to be quite honest. And that in itself has brought me towards the occupation that I'm in. And I think also that for me, a lot of us introverted types and they just want to work behind the scene, in the hospital; they don't want to see people. I'm not afraid of working with people, and that's probably one of my fortes, and to shaping the successful path so far of my mobile business, it's been built on my relationships, and I think that that's been largely shaped by tragedy.

DIEDERIK: When did you start to look at the business side of veterinary practice, and separate it from the clinical side?

ARI: I was starting to look at that in the job that I had before I started my mobile business. I'm not a businessman, and perhaps I'm being hard on myself, but saying that to myself doesn't help me become a businessman. I was looking at more management stuff in the previous practice but I didn't really get very far with that, and really, I had to look at it when I started up my mobile business.

That was when the business side of things came to the fore, out of necessity more than anything else. That's been probably the single biggest challenge in my veterinary career from the time I started the mobile business, and it's still an ongoing challenge for me.

DIEDERIK: Our industry, as you eluded to before, has a 'reputation'. What do you think has kept you sane?

ARI: There are two components to that. There's an internal factor, that you either have more or less of, and because some people just have a predisposition to running themselves down into the ground.

And there's the external factors. What's kept me sane, I think, is partly just my drive, wanting to perform, wanting to be the best vet that I can be, or having this thing in my head that I have some ability and I get such satisfaction from doing the job that's helped me to keep going in times of struggle. And I also had a fantastic mentor when I graduated, I had two fantastic mentors. One was my partner – well, she wasn't my partner at the time, we were sort of on and off a bit, now my wife – and the other was a vet mentor, who was the head of vet school at the time.

Having her on the end of the phone and having my wife on the end of the phone absolutely no doubt kept me sane. I would have gotten burnt down without those two, there's no doubt about it. I was 31 when I graduated, and I still spent the first six months crying. But you know, perhaps, there's a difference, like a 21- or 22-year-old, they'd probably struggle, but maybe not so many of them would start crying because at that age, you've still got this 'I can do anything attitude', and you've got this 'I want people to think I can do anything attitude'. So, at 31 years old, I was able to have that support, and I've always been able to see the bigger picture, and that is that the bigger picture is that you do what you can.

DIEDERIK: What's the biggest thing you've given back to your community?

ARI: The biggest thing I've given back is just to be a thoughtful caring person in the community, and trying to make a difference on the little world, by smiling at people and by engaging with people and not shying away from trying your hardest to...just be a thoughtful person.

DIEDERIK: What's your vision for the future of the veterinary industry?

ARI: My ideal vision for the veterinary industry is one where there's a lot more respect in the industry and where actually vets as a whole are given much more credentials to provide services both in the veterinary world and non-veterinary.

I think the veterinary industry will always have the small providers for the people down the street who just want to have pets in their family and get on with their lives and have beautiful large extended families, with furry and non-furry members. And, I see... one of my biggest fears for the veterinary industry are these large corporate entities.

DIEDERIK: During your career, was there ever a turning point, a snap point, a line in the sand, a defining moment at which you said, 'enough is enough'?

ARI: For me that's a bit of a no-brainer, because I was one of the first mobile clinics. And now, mobile vets are becoming a genuine professional entity in themselves, and for me, you have to be that. That turning point was when my wife and I, we agreed on a mobile practice, my general job came to an abrupt end, and I had to make decisions, and I got my mobile business fully up and running within two months in terms of having everything setup, the van, the website set up, and two months later I was a mobile vet. It has really gone from strength to strength in many ways, and there's still a lot to learn.

And that would have been the magic turning point really, going from the average usual practicing, employed vet to a mobile vet, sort of starting in a different industry.

DIEDERIK: That's a perfect point on which to stop. Ari, thank you very much.

Key Take-Aways

- Make a 'business' plan when you graduate so that you know what your first few years will be like
- Look for a first job in a practice that will support you and interview them as hard as they interview you
- Success is a balance of career and family
- It is essential to have a few great mentors who are there for you in times of trouble and who you can bounce ideas off when times are tough
- The veterinary business is all about being able to communicate

> **"Working with pets and people is a privilege – is that how you're treating it?"**
>
> Diederik Gelderman

Dr Barbara Fougere

Dr Barbara Fougere

BSc BVMS (Hons) MODT BHSc (CMed) MHSc (Herb Med) Grad Dip VA Grad Dip VCHM
Grad Dip VWHM CVA (IVAS) CVBM CVCP CMAVA

> *"If a dog jumps in your lap, it is because he is fond of you; but if a cat does the same thing, it is because you lap is warmer."*
>
> ~ Alfred North Whitehead

Barbara graduated from Sydney University in 1987 and practises in Sydney Australia at All Natural Vet Care. She works exclusively in the field of veterinary integrative medicine. She is the CEO of the College of Integrative Therapies and one of its faculty members. She has served on numerous professional boards and is currently the chairperson for the American College Veterinary Botanical Medicine working to have herbal medicine recognised at Diplomate level. She holds a Master's degree in Herbal Medicine and a Bachelor's degree in Complementary Medicine as well as a Master's in the field of education and training. She has authored two books and co-authored two veterinary texts *Veterinary Herbal Medicine* (2007) and *Integrating Complementary Medicine into Veterinary Practice* (2008).

? DIEDERIK: Barbara, what ignited your passion to be a vet, and at what age did that happen?

... BARBARA: It was pretty early on. I remember my father scoring a sheep and pulling out the innards, and I found that fascinating. And, as a child, having some animals that had been injured, hit by a car, taking them to the vet and seeing what a veterinarian did to bring my cat back to life basically. That inspired me and it just seemed like a natural thing to do.

And the other thing was, I didn't know what other things were out there.

DIEDERIK: You — no pun intended — went into an alternative career path. How did that happen?

BARBARA: Within my first two years of practice, I became disillusioned with what I was doing. I was working in a very large practice, working stupid hours, getting burnt out really quickly, fundamentally feeling *"Is this all there to it? Is this what I'm meant to be doing?"* I felt frustrated that there were some things that I couldn't treat, that some people didn't want to go through with the diagnosis. And, I was saving up to go travelling, and it just so happened that I joined Qantas as an international flight attendant. I continued to study, business, economics, Japanese Economics. I also studied homeopathy. I was searching for what is my next step, and it wasn't until I got tired of flying, that I joined 'industry'.

I went from a Yves Saint Laurent uniform and high shoes to gumboots and green overalls looking after endoparasiticides in sheep and cattle and a small range of companion animal products. That's when I got interested in training, and so then I went on and did a Master's in education.

Each step of the way, I've had experiences that have steered me in a particular direction. I've always kept a hand in practice. Even when I was flying in Qantas, I worked part-time for a practice in Sydney.

DIEDERIK: And then you transitioned into an alternative medicine practice. How did that come about?

BARBARA: From working with sheep and cattle, I was recruited into a pet food company, where I became very interested in nutrition. I just continued to study, for about 25 years, I love studying and learning. I started studying acupuncture when I was working in industry. I was doing locum work around Sydney and I realised that there weren't any practices that I could go into and do these things. I thought; you know, no one's doing this. I want to do it, I want to be able to offer people other treatment options for difficult and challenging conditions, and I setup a physical practice in 2003, but I was doing house calls for a couple of years before then.

That's when I found my home, my passion. I'd spent all those years searching, thinking *"Gosh, what is it that I really need to be doing? What is it that I want to do?"* and I had to create it. I had to create the type of practice, the type of medicine that I wanted to practice.

I feel very excited about practice, there's not a day that goes by where I don't think, *"Wow, that worked. That's amazing."* And it's that sense of *"This is what I'm meant to be doing. I'm getting challenging cases that are stimulating and interesting, and I'm actually able to do something about it."* And that's what Integrated Medicine means to me.

? DIEDERIK: What didn't they teach you at Uni that you now know is essential to being a successful veterinarian?

BARBARA: We come out of University where you have all the wiz bang gadgets and clients that are willing to spend more because they're coming to see the University with challenging problems. We have this expectation when we graduate that everything's going to be easy to diagnose, and we're going to have all the tools at our fingertips and we're going to be able to treat this patient. The reality is, clients don't necessarily want to spend the money, or there's some situations where you simply can't make a diagnosis. What I've learned is that the diagnosis isn't actually the most important thing about. We're always taught that diagnosis was the key and then you treat them according to protocol. What I found out is we don't really learn a hell a lot of about health and how to improve health and maintenance. The standard paradigm is you vaccinate, you put chemicals on the animal every month, we give oral substances every month and we give them a commercial pet food every day. That's what we consider to be health, and it's not that at all. We don't get taught about how to maintain and optimise health through good nutrition. I'm talking about nutrition at a cellular level, and real food diets. We don't get taught how to feed animals naturally. We don't get taught about strategic parasite control. At University, we rely too heavily on products and not on educating clients about environmental control.

We really don't get a basis in how to treat chronic disease and optimise health, and that's something that is missing.

DIEDERIK: Very interesting. What are two or three things that a newly graduated vet needs to do immediately to get their career turbocharged?

BARBARA: I would recommend investing in your education. Just because you've left the University, that's not – you're only just starting to learn. Decide what areas you're interested in and go for it.

The second thing is to volunteer. Get on some committees, even if it's just one committee with your local AVA branch, or something to do with your profession. You're going to meet other practitioners who could become your mentor. You don't feel so isolated in practice.

The third thing is to create some boundaries around your work life so that you learn how to say no, because it's very, very easy to burn out in your first couple of years.

DIEDERIK: If you were starting again, would you be a vet?

BARBARA: Yeah. Absolutely. It's a terrific career.

DIEDERIK: What were three major challenges you faced in your career?

BARBARA: In my first two years of practice I felt compromised ethically. That's something you need to get on top of pretty early. Reflect on what's going on in your practice, what's going on in your professional life and decide if that is something that you can cope with or not. Sometimes there are pressures put on you as a young graduate, and if you feel uncomfortable with it, I think you've got to stand up and say no, or offer an alternative.

The other major one was dealing with euthanasia. It affected me deeply from early on. It was the most challenging time for me. I wasn't clinically diagnosed as depressed, but I could see how easily you could go into depression. Just being aware of it and being able to talk to other people about it, helps you create an awareness, and once you're aware of that, change it. If there's something like that happening, speak to people, don't keep it in yourself. Seek counselling if you need to.

The third is being a female in a male-orientated profession. I was branded as a feminist early on in my career when I thought I was just being a humanist and pointing out the obvious disparities between males and females in the profession.

DIEDERIK: How did you manage to have a balanced personal life and career?

BARBARA: I don't think I've done it very well at times. I'm a lot better at it now than I was. If you fail to plan, you plan to fail. Start up by setting some priorities, the things that are important to you in life, and then that becomes like your mission statement about what it is to be you. Then, make sure that you create time, you create space for family and friends. Your family and friends and health are the most important part of your life. If you think anybody's going to thank you when you have a heart attack because you're overworked and tired...

I know it's hard, I know when at the end of the day, you're about to go home, somebody rings up, there's a patient in crisis, you feel compelled to *"Okay, well, bring it in straight away"*, and you know you're going to be there for the next three to four hours that night. You don't have to hang on to everything, let go of some of that, and then you'll have the space for the important things in life; your health, your mental health and your family and friends.

DIEDERIK: Well said. What does success look like to you?

BARBARA: Success is doing what it is that you love to do so that you don't feel like it's work, that it's something that you enjoy and being inspired and motivated. And having the luxury of that, having the luxury of not feeling like you have to go to work,

And then health and family and friends. The combination of family and friendships and the work that you enjoy doing, being healthy, that to me is wealth. Wealth is anything that you want to find, but you can have a lot of money and have very poor health or very poor relationships and be unhappy. So, to me, success isn't about having wealth; it's health and work that you enjoy doing.

DIEDERIK: You've always been motivated and 'up', how do you maintain that?

BARBARA: Because I've found what I'm passionate about. I'm so inspired and not a day goes by when I don't learn something. If you can find something that you feel very passionate about, and it may not be your work as a veterinarian, it may actually be something outside of your career that you feel passionate about, but that's what keeps you really motivated and inspired.

DIEDERIK: If you had the chance to do it all again. Is there anything you'd do differently?

BARBARA: I've thought about that because sometimes I feel like I wasted several years, but when I look back I think *"No, I didn't waste anything."* Everything that I learned and did has actually come to fruition with what I'm doing now.

DIEDERIK: You've achieved a heck of a lot. What do you believe holds most vets back from achieving their goals?

BARBARA: I have a belief in abundance, that there's plenty out there rather than scarcity. And that's an important distinction because if you start off thinking there is enough, you don't get caught up in greed or get caught up in thinking of poor me, or like I won't charge the client that much money because I don't deserve it.

I write down goals; I've got a list of goals on the refrigerator at home. I know that not all those goals are going to get done this year, but if I don't write it down, none of it will get done. I get a sense of achievement when I can tick stuff off the list.

You can't do everything, but pick the things that are important and go for it. And you can manifest it; if you really have a mindset, if you visualise what it is that you want. And that's an important meditation, I think, is to actually take the time to think *"What is it that's really important to me? What is it that I see myself doing in five years' time or ten years' time?"* And if you try to visualise it, it's a really powerful technique to have a vision of what it is that you want to be doing or how you want it be. And then, all your decision making subconsciously and consciously can steer you towards making that a reality.

So, I think you create your own reality.

DIEDERIK: There are a few people who have said similar things, but none have phrased it as well as you. I think that'll give people a lot more insight to a success mindset.

If you were helping a new graduate, what pitfalls are you going to suggest that they avoid?

BARBARA: Setting boundaries with clients. When something goes wrong with a client in the practice, it can really have multiple effects on your psyche. If something goes wrong, that then becomes overwhelming, it can take up a lot of your headspace, a lot of your energy. And, you forget about the other 20 people, the 20 patients that you've helped. So, the negatives can be overwhelming. That's one of the things to learn very early on is that you do the best job you can, you're not going to get everything right. You're going to make some mistakes. Be kind to yourself, learn from your mistakes.

From a client communication point of view; set some boundaries. If you feel that someone has been rude to you, call them out on it – politely say *"Look, I don't feel comfortable with this discussion. Perhaps you'd be better off seeing another veterinarian."* And they'll often go, *"Oh, sorry. I didn't mean it like that,"* or whatever. They'll back right down. If you don't set that boundary, they'll walk all over you.

There are some people that will try it on, and that could also be staff members that you work with, or bosses, or colleagues. Call them out on it, stand up to it, be polite and just set your boundaries.

DIEDERIK: Has luck or tragedy had any part in getting you where you are today?

NOTE: You can find Barbara's answer to this question and the remainder of this interview online at:

www.VeterinarySuccessSecretsRevealed.com

Key Take-Aways

- Make sure that you create some boundaries around your work life so that you learn how to say no and take care of yourself

- Sometimes there are pressures put on you as a young graduate, and if you feel uncomfortable with it, you've got to stand up and say no

- Success to me is doing what it is that you love to do so that you don't feel like it's work and have good relationships and good health

- Staying sane is about having your boundaries and being true to yourself

- I have a belief in abundance, that there's plenty out there for everyone rather than scarcity

> **"The 'Why' is the reason why your practice exists and it's the reason why your team come to work. And the 'Why' COMES FROM the leader – s/he defines it and shares it. It's not the 'How' or the 'What' that defines why they come to work and why your business exists, it's the 'Why'."**
>
> Diederik Gelderman

Dr David Stasiuk

Dr David Stasiuk

BVSc, MBA

> *"There are two means of refuge from the miseries of life: music and cats."*
>
> ~ Albert Schweitzer

He was influenced early on by the adventures of James Herriot and Gerald Durrell and completed his Bachelor of Veterinary Science with the University of Melbourne in 1999. David started practicing as a mixed animal vet in South-Eastern Victoria.

In 2001 David travelled to the UK and worked in several veterinary hospitals. During this time he became a member of the Royal College of Veterinary Surgeons.

Since returning to Australia, David has worked with several small animal clinics in Melbourne and completed a post-graduate a MBA (Monash 2006).

In February 2010 David joined his friend, Dr David Wilson, and purchased Cheltenham Veterinary Clinic.

David is married to Anna and they have three daughters. David enjoys travelling, reading, and endurance sports.

DIEDERIK: What ignited your passion to become a vet, and at what age did that happen David?

DAVID: It was pretty clear. I was in grade 2 and I had my crayons and I drew a picture of Dr Stasiuk, age 22, and a massive syringe, dripping blood, and I was standing on the consult table with a dog and I think that really helped give me a goal throughout my primary and senior school years to achieve this dream.

DIEDERIK: What didn't they teach you at the University that you now know is absolutely crucial to your success as a practicing veterinarian?

DAVID: University prepared us to be technically brilliant, disciplined to study and complete all those exams.

What they don't teach you, which is critical when you get out, is how to talk to people, how to communicate in trying to achieve what's best for the animal. It sort of comes down to sales in that respect.

And then business. You tend to do your MBA (on the job) when you start a business, that's probably the best way of doing it. That's been a good learning curve, and certainly reiterates that you should just get into it and throw your hat in the ring and just start doing what you want to do and you can learn along the way.

The biggest thing is people skills, dealing with clients, dealing with employees, dealing with each other and being in a collective business where you're a team, not just the individual vet working hard to achieve what they think is the best for the animal.

DIEDERIK: What did they teach you at University that retrospectively, you know is incorrect?

DAVID: Not so much incorrect, it's just application of the skills they taught us, especially communication skills.

DIEDERIK: Based on your experience, what are three things that a new graduate needs to do as soon as possible to turbocharge their career?

DAVID: Your first job is crucial to building momentum. Find a supportive clinic which has a group of people, or even an individual that you can relate to and you can share and learn off. A mentor is critical.

Finding a good supportive clinic which accepts that you're a new graduate, that you don't know everything there is to know in clinical practice, and to help lay down a pathway for you to follow and teach you the skills you need to learn about surgery, consulting, but also business.

? DIEDERIK: What are a couple of things that a new graduate needs to avoid doing as soon as they graduate to make sure that they get on track?

DAVID: You certainly don't want to enter the first job that comes along and end up in a toxic environment with a bad team, no support.

Secondly, trying to just find that balance in life where you've got your work but also, you've got your friends and family, hobbies outside of work so that you can unwind and de-stress, because there is no doubt, the first 12 months is going to be an emotional and physical rollercoaster for a new graduate.

? DIEDERIK: What were three major challenges that you faced?

DAVID: When I graduated, dealing with clients in the consult room. You go from having no real interaction with anyone except your partner, family and friends and Uni friends, to having to talk to 30–50 strangers every day that you interact with, that you need to build confidence with and create a good impression that allows them to trust you. That's something that you need to learn.

? DIEDERIK: Any other challenges that you had?

DAVID: Working with people.

Working hard into a lot of after-hours, so trying to find that balance. If you just keep putting everything into work, it can be suffocating and quite depressing at times.

There's a lot of compassion fatigue, but you don't know about that until you start practicing, and there's no way you can prepare for it, unless you've spoken to someone who can give you the tools to help deal with those challenges of, the three euthanasias you might do in a day or the client that's upset with you and calls you names. How do you deal with that?

DIEDERIK: If you were starting again, would you in fact be a vet?

DAVID: I would, absolutely. Especially now in retrospect, 15 years later, having built a successful business and working the hours I work, taking the holidays when I take them and having family time. The career has given me that.

DIEDERIK: You mentioned balance a little bit earlier. How did you manage to balance family, career and fatherhood?

DAVID: On graduating, I quickly realised that all my time was spent working and worrying about work. And so, I quickly took up team sports, basketball, I took up life-drawing and I took up music again, lots of running and cycling, a lot of good times with friends and family, so getting out and going on holidays and planning concerts and parties and things like that. So, trying to organise my extracurricular life. That was very useful.

DIEDERIK: What does success look like to you?

DAVID: Success, the freedom to make choices. Having a business, I've now got choices. I have a lot of challenges but I have choices to work when I want to work, to holiday, to choose which team members I want to work with, what team members we have, what type of clinic, how I consult, how I want to be perceived. I think choice, to me, is success. You could say freedom, but again, freedom might imply I want to get away from it, but I don't.

② DIEDERIK: If you had to pick one or two successes, what would be the biggest ones you'd pick?

… DAVID: The day my baby was born. In veterinary, it would have to be, graduating the course. That's a massive milestone. You've absolutely flogged yourself to get there. Getting your first job seems to be a success, but it may not be. Certainly, acquiring my first clinic, I think that was a huge success. It did take two years of searching around to find that, but that patience paid off and the grit paid off.

Having the confidence to pull it off and take on employees and all those responsibilities of dealing with a team.

② DIEDERIK: Would you pick one or two keys to those successes?

… DAVID: Common keys; if you know what you want, that's the first step. Then having the self-confidence to move on that desire. Speaking to people that are doing what you want to, they're already there. Speaking to them is critical, so a cup of coffee, phone call, if they're into Skype, yeah, you can Skype. Get to meet people that are doing what you want to do, and finding the mentor who can help you get there. So, what's the road map? How am I going to get from A to B. Then learning how to be a good leader. How to deal with people and lead people.

② DIEDERIK: You're always motivated, focused. How do you stay like that?

… DAVID: I eat well. I think having a goal in mind. Where do I want to go? What do I want to do? Why do I want to do it? It comes back to the 'Why', which is a pretty famous question, that 'Why'!

Finding that balance of work, satisfaction, with family satisfaction and physical satisfaction, it's just that balance.

DIEDERIK: If you had the chance to do it all again, is there anything you'd do differently?

DAVID: I would have liked to have started the veterinary clinic business side a lot earlier. I think I was 34 when I started.

So, yeah, probably time, just getting in early. If you know what you want to do, just get on with it.

DIEDERIK: When did you make the differentiation between the business side of vet and the non-business side?

DAVID: When I was getting paid $35,000 a year to work 60 hours, and I heard business owners getting paid $160 grand plus in the early 90s. To me, that was a question of 'why' and 'how do they do it'. And yeah, I sort of went in to look at learning business skills with the MBA at Monash in 2004. That was early in the piece, but again, I felt like I was probably too young and inexperienced when really, I should have just gone for it. So, then I waited another six years before I got on with acquiring a clinic and getting on with completing my goal and moving forward with what I wanted.

DIEDERIK: What do you think holds most vets back from achieving their goals?

DAVID: You can get distracted these days with anything. You can have a bad day in the office and you want to quit. But I think if you've got the why and you focus and you have a written goal, a one-year goal, three-, five-, ten-year goals; the longer the better. If you have something that you can strive for...nine out of ten times, you're going to hold to that course. You're going to complete it. You need to have that long-term view.

DIEDERIK: Interesting. Documented goals. And I guess that's common knowledge, but not many people put that into action.

DAVID: No, it's surprising actually. The goals that work really well for me were the quarterly milestone, so it's quarterly 90-day goals, but also having the one-year overview. So, being able to chunk it into smaller bite-sized pieces so that it's achievable, and that's been really powerful.

DIEDERIK: Do you think that tragedy or luck has played any part in you achieving what you've achieved?

DAVID: No tragedy. No luck, just determination. Just getting on with it. If you want something, set that goal and figure out how to get there, and if you need someone like a mentor to help you, then do that.

DIEDERIK: If you were helping someone else starting out, what pitfalls would you tell them they need to avoid?

DAVID: As a new graduate, finding the job that suits them in an environment and team that suites them. It's probably the most critical one.

Don't be persuaded by the difference in salary or car or location. The most important thing is the people you're going to work with. You may not be able to figure that out in one interview, but you can certainly spend some time with them to work that out. And maybe, again, working with your mentor to give feedback and discuss whether or not it's going to be a good fit for you.

DIEDERIK: Our industry has a certain reputation, what do you think has kept you sane?

DAVID: When I come home from work, there's nothing veterinary about my home except for the dog and cats and guinea pigs and the fish. Having family and friends that are outside of that circle has been really good to help me, just because they have all their own other problems and interests and I can get involved with those, and it's refreshing. Also sport, coming back to physical exertion and exercise. To me, just being able to switch off to avoid that compassion fatigue, to manage the worry that your veterinary career, your work, might induce.

DIEDERIK: What's the biggest thing that you've given back to your community?

DAVID: I've given out plenty of jobs, managing all the staff and giving them a nice place to work. Making it a nice place, not just a job, but a nice place that employees want to come to and feel like they're a valued member and that they're making a difference. I'm lucky to have that at the moment. Nurses who are proud of everything that they do. The feedback they get, they let me know straight away. If someone said something nice, they tell us, and if they've done something they reckon that's good, or they have an idea, they tell us.

DIEDERIK: What do you consider to be three key drivers to success in vet?

NOTE: You can find David's answer to this question and the remainder of this interview online at:

www.VeterinarySuccessSecretsRevealed.com

Key Take-Aways

- You tend to do your MBA (on the job), when you start a business, and that's the best way of doing it

- Find a supportive clinic which has a group of people, or even an individual that you can relate to and you can share and learn from – mentoring is critical

- You can imagine your daughter asking you, *"Daddy, why didn't you just do what you wanted to do?" "Well, I couldn't be bothered. I was watching a good movie and there were too many distractions."*

- If you want something, set that goal and figure out how to get there

- The goals that work well are the quarterly 90-day goals, but also having the one-year overview

> **"Leaders who succeed in creating a practice that lives its 'Why' in all that it does, will have the unquestionable and undying loyalty of those that mirror those same beliefs and by that, I mean staff and clients."**
>
> Diederik Gelderman

Dr Debbie Delahunty

Dr Debbie Delahunty

BVSc(Hons) & CertIV PractMgt (Vet)

> *"An animal's eyes have the power to speak a great language."* ~ Martin Buber

Debbie works in and owns Horsham (Horsham Veterinary Clinic), Victoria. She was born and grew up in Sydney. She attended the University of Sydney, completing her BVSc(Hons) in 1987.

Debbie left Sydney to work in dairy practice but ended up in Western Victoria. Initially she worked half the week each for two different practices. She ended up full-time in Horsham and ultimately bought the practice in 1991.

In 1993 Debbie and her husband built a purpose-built hospital which achieved ASAVA Hospital of Excellence accreditation shortly after. The team of two vets and two support staff has now grown to a staff of sixteen.

Debbie was on the committee of the AVPMA and is a founding member of the AVBA and a past president. She is passionate about helping others develop and grow their businesses as well as doing what she can to help raise the standards of practice of the entire industry.

Her key success is her beautiful family. She is also extremely proud of her Veterinary Hospital team and says that she could not ask for a more dedicated, fun and competent group of people to work with.

DIEDERIK: Debbie, what ignited your passion to become a vet and at what age did you make the decision?

DEBBIE: As long as I can remember, my ambition was to either be a vet, a zookeeper or an astronaut. For as long as I can remember I wanted to be a vet or do something with animals. I was always nagging for more pets, trying to get dogs to follow me home, and telling my parents they were strays.

DIEDERIK: What didn't they teach you at Uni that you know retrospectively is crucial to becoming a good practitioner?

DEBBIE: What they did teach me was how to look for challenging medical cases and how to work those through. But when I first went into practice, I had no idea what a vaccine protocol was, had no idea about skin allergies and the common, the simple things. And I didn't realise that so much of my day would be spent doing routine things and not finding those complex cases.

The other thing is communication skills. It doesn't matter how good a vet you are, if you can't communicate well with your clients, then they don't appreciate your skills. We had no training in how to conduct a consultation, how to explain to clients appropriately what we're going to do to their animals.

The last thing is business understanding, which at the beginning for me wasn't such a big deal, but once I owned my own practice, I struggled with how little I knew. I know it's not practical to teach undergraduates how to run a business, but giving them some basic understanding, and in particular how an associate vet contributes to the success of the business is something that I think could have been very helpful for me when I first graduated.

DIEDERIK: Was there anything that they did teach you that in the hard light of veterinary business has been proven to be incorrect?

DEBBIE: I would have said the high standards from University were impractical for the real world. But, more and more, I've come to change my opinion, because it used to be a given that what was done at University couldn't possibly happen in the real world. But, I don't believe that anymore.

We're in a country town, and we practice a very high standard of care, we're an ASAVA Accredited hospital. And, yes, we don't have access to some of the diagnostic equipment that a University has, but many of our clients are very happy to be referred for that.

DIEDERIK: There's a new graduate sitting in front of you, what are two or three things you're going to tell them that they've got to do immediately to turbocharge their career?

DEBBIE: Find a practice which supports the highest standard of quality care. Don't settle for going somewhere where corners are cut.

Take responsibility for your own development. Don't expect to be hand held. Mentoring is very important. But, the realities of practice are that you can't have someone by your side the whole time. Do understand your limitations but also don't be afraid to have a go and if you don't know, grab a text book, work it out and ask people. Make sure you push your own development yourself.

The third thing; go and work in a country or regional practice. You get a vast range of experience which leads to more opportunities to have a go. And particularly with after-hours' work, you get some exciting cases.

DIEDERIK: Same new graduate, what are two or three things you're going to tell them to avoid if they want to get ahead quickly?

DEBBIE: Avoid joining a practice that doesn't sit right with your personal values, because then, you're only going to be a square peg in a round hole. That probably means you have to examine your own values, what's important to you in your professional life.

A mistake I've seen new graduates make is treating nurses and support staff poorly, or with condescension. They deserve respect because they're professionals. And quite often, they know a lot more than a new graduate does, so make them your friends. Accept the support that they can give, and treat them with respect.

The third one, is avoid pretending that you know things you don't, and don't be afraid to ask question and don't be afraid to admit your mistakes, and that applies to your fellow workers and your clients. Honesty is always respected.

DIEDERIK: If you were starting again, would you be a vet?

DEBBIE: Absolutely. Though, there are times when my answer may not have been so empathic. I've been through times of burnout and wondering why am I doing this. In fact, I can't image doing anything else.

DIEDERIK: What were three major challenges that you faced?

DEBBIE: The biggest was balancing motherhood and the long hours that I needed to work in a practice that was still developing and establishing itself. And I always thought with that guilt, when we're not at home with kids. We feel guilty for working. And, when you own a business, when you're at home with the kids, you feel guilty for not being there running the business.

There certainly were times where my business has gone through some pretty tough financial times. A lot of it in the early days when we just didn't know how to manage it properly.

Building our purpose-built hospital; the whole building process was a challenging time. Trying to keep running a business and manage a building site.

❓ DIEDERIK: How did you end up balancing family and motherhood?

💬 DEBBIE: It was made easier by the fact that my husband was a farmer and was able to be flexible in his working hours. Being in the country, once my daughters were at high school, it was just around the corner, they could walk to work if I couldn't get there to pick them up.

There were times that I really resented work for taking me away from my kids. But, as my daughters have grown older, it's certainly lowered that stress, but even now there are still times when I am frustrated when I have to work on weekends and there's something that I'd rather be doing with the family. There were many times where I chose to employ more vets than I probably needed just so that I could have more time at home, and so we did make some financial sacrifices in that way.

❓ DIEDERIK: What does success look like to you?

💬 DEBBIE: I've always jokingly said that when I can take myself off the after-hours', I will have achieved the highest pinnacle of success, and I still haven't gotten there quite yet.

There does have to be a financial aspect to success, but for me, that's not the be all and end all, but it has to be a level of financial success out of the business, so that I can educate my kids the way I want to, I want to be able to travel and just feel financially secure.

The biggest thing is just having a well-run business with a happy team, where we come to work each day and 99% of the time, people are happy to be here and we enjoy what we do, we feel proud of what we do, we're respected in our community. And that's just as important, if not more important than the financial success.

DIEDERIK: What do you think is or are your biggest successes to date?

DEBBIE: My team. We have a really great staff, vets, nurses, receptionist, groomers, practice manager, the whole lot. We've worked to develop a good team, we put a lot of time into training and education of our staff, and that's paid off.

DIEDERIK: You are a motivated person what are the methods that you use to keep you motivated and focused?

DEBBIE: I definitely have had times of burnout. I've learned over the years that I need take some time off, and this is advice I was given by Dr Jim Stowe, a Canadian practice consultant. He came in and did some work with us many years ago. I was not taking holidays, I was working long hours, and I was pretty over the whole thing. He said, *"Look, you just have to have holidays, even if you don't go anywhere or do anything, just take time away from the practice. It will survive without you."* And I absolutely did. Knowing my own limitations, knowing that if I keep pushing too hard, I will burn out. I do know that giving myself time away from the practice is really important and I can recharge and stay focused.

And my involvement with the Australian Veterinary Business Association; it was an opportunity for me to get together with people doing the same thing that I am. I gained a lot of inspiration from those people, so surrounding yourself with other motivated, enthusiastic people helps as well.

DIEDERIK: If you had the chance to do it all again, is there anything you'd do differently?

DEBBIE: Perhaps if I knew what I was getting into when I bought the business. In the early days, I may not have done that. But now, yes, I'm happy that I own the business, but there were times when it was pretty grim and financially challenging. I'd definitely would have gotten business training, help and learned management skills much earlier than I did.

DIEDERIK: You're in a bit of unique practice. You're a rural practice, and you started off doing a lot of cattle and sheep work as well as the small animal work. You eventually got rid of the large animal component?

DEBBIE: Horsham had quite a bit of a beef cattle industry when I first came here (1988). There's still sheep work, quite a bit of horse. Gradually, the farming changed from livestock to cropping. So, that side of our business was declining and it was when Jim Stowe was here during his consultancy that one of his recommendations was for us to cease doing large animal work, because it was down to a very small percentage of our turnover but it was creating a lot of our challenges and conflicts.

The other struggle; you need to lead by your values, and my values were always to provide high quality. I was finding it harder and harder to deliver that quality to our large animal clients because it was hard to employ vets who wanted large animal work when we did such a small amount. So, it was not sitting well with me that we weren't delivering the kind of service that I wanted to deliver. And, it never occurred to me to just say, *"No, we don't do it,"* until Jim Stowe said *"Why not? Send all your clients a letter."* It was quite tough because I enjoy the large animal work, but I just didn't want to do it all. It was a tough emotional decision, but it has been the right decision for us to make.

DIEDERIK: Do you think that tragedy or luck has played any part in you achieving your success?

DEBBIE: Maybe a little bit of luck, but it's been a lot more hard work and sweat. Yes, my boss was ready to sell when he was and things like that have worked in our favour. But, really, there's been a lot more blood, sweat and tears, than luck and tragedy.

DIEDERIK: If you were helping someone else, what pitfalls should they avoid?

DEBBIE: Avoid not setting your pricing correctly, that was our big mistake, and that proved to be a totally incorrect assumption. Charge appropriately, properly and fairly for what you do. From a personal management point of view, take time out away from the practice to give yourself some breathing time and to recharge the batteries.

DIEDERIK: What's your passion?

DEBBIE: Continuing to raise our standards. So, we have a lot of written procedures. I love seeing our quality improve all the time.

DIEDERIK: You've got a perspective on the business side of practice versus the clinical side, when did you make that distinction?

NOTE: You can find Debbie's answer to this question and the remainder of this interview online at:

www.VeterinarySuccessSecretsRevealed.com

Key Take-Aways

- It doesn't matter how good a vet you are, if you can't communicate well with your clients, then they don't appreciate your skills

- You need to live by your values and work in a practice that has your values

- My passion is most definitely continuing to raise our standards

- Treat people well, both your clients and your staff – they are what make your practice. Treat them like you'd like to be treated

- There's always something to learn, and as soon as you start to coast, then you're going to slip behind. So, ensure you continue your education in both businesses and in your technical work

> **"As an industry, we're brilliant at getting better patient outcomes, but what we're really bad at is charging adequately for our time and expertise in achieving those outcomes and understanding how valued and valuable those outcomes are for the pet owner and that they are happy to pay us what we deserve for achieving those outcomes for them."**
>
> Diederik Gelderman

Dr Gary Turnbull

Dr Gary Turnbull

BVSc (Hons) 1995

> *"Every boy should have two things: a dog, and a mother willing to let him have one"* ~ Anonymous

Gary is a Principal of the Lincoln Institute, a boutique leadership development company delivering facilitated training and coaching to a broad range of allied health professions, including the veterinary profession. He is a highly recognised and respected speaker and facilitator in the fields of veterinary practice management and leadership, veterinary business models and life-balance strategies. Gary delivered the 2015 AVBA 'On the Move' Series, *Leading Change in your Practice*. He also developed the Goldmine Veterinary Dental Program which he has presented internationally.

Gary is also the director of the East Port Veterinary Hospital, a multi-award winning business and an Australian Small Animal Veterinary Association Accredited *Hospital of Excellence* situated on the mid-north coast of New South Wales. He is a first-class honours graduate from the University of Sydney and a Chartered Member of the Australian Veterinary Association. He is also a member of the Australian Small Animal Veterinary Association, Australian Veterinary Business Association and Australian Veterinary Dental Society.

Gary is married with three children and resides in Port Macquarie, Australia.

DIEDERIK: Gary, what ignited your passion to become a vet, and at what age did that start?

GARY: As an early teenager, I had an interest in the medical sciences. I was drawn to human medicine, veterinary medicine and dentistry. Then I knew it was vet.

DIEDERIK: You went on a non-traditional journey. Can you share a little of that?

GARY: I graduated in 1995. My first job was in a small animal practice in Sydney. The owner of the practice had recently purchased both practices I was working in. She was around for about my first three months to mentor me, and she was a good mentor from a clinical perspective. But after about three months, I was left to run the practice and she moved away.

So, at 23, I was looking at veterinary practice from an economic perspective. I had a fairly sound understanding of the financial realities of veterinary practice within 12 months of starting.

That lead to me wanting my own practice. So, after two-and-a-half years, and as a result of 'cold calling' practices in the area that I wanted to move to, someone, said, *"Yup, I'm interested,"* and within 12 months or so, my wife (also a veterinarian), and I had purchased a practice.

That was about 2000. It was a one and a half vets and two support staff practice. That grew rapidly. We did a massive renovation to move to a purpose built ASAVA accredited facility. We were awarded AVA Hospital of Excellence accreditation in 2007. It was then that I started to be mentored. I then moved to a series of mentors that led me to where I am now.

? DIEDERIK: You now coach, mentor, train leadership in non-vet as well as in vet, don't you?

GARY: We train practice owners, managers and senior people in the veterinary and paramedical professions – the business models are so similar and the leadership principles we teach are principle based so they apply across industries.

? DIEDERIK: What didn't they teach you at vet school that you now know is crucial to being a good veterinarian?

GARY: What they didn't teach us is that you spend much more time working with people than you do with animals. By that I mean the team in which you work and of course the general public. We had zero training in preparation for dealing with the public.

And the work we do is, at times, emotionally charged and emotionally challenging. We were totally under-prepared to deal with that.

? DIEDERIK: What did they teach you at vet school that you now know to be incorrect?

GARY: What they taught is academic medicine. In an ideal world, this is what we would do, but it's not an ideal world and we have to work with people, the public's expectations, their limitations, their emotions. So, what we were taught from a clinical perspective is not necessarily always practically applicable.

? DIEDERIK: What are three things you're going to tell a new graduate that they've got to do to turbocharge themselves immediately?

GARY: #1; they need to change their communication. They've learned the medical language. And that's the language that their colleagues understand and their mentors understand, but it's not a language that the general public understands.

#2; get comfortable with the notion that they're in sales. Whether you like it or not, you are selling a diagnosis, a diagnostic plan, a treatment plan, you're selling yourself, you're selling the practice that you're working for. We are in the world of selling all day, every day. Selling is a good thing because all we're doing is helping people out; ethically helping people in need.

#3; value themselves. The more we stop thinking about charging based on our time and think about charging based on the value that we add to the client, their family, that is somewhat of a paradigm shift.

DIEDERIK: The other side, three things you're going to tell them to avoid doing?

GARY: #1; avoid taking it home. One of the biggest challenges is switching off. At the end of the day, it is a job and we want to have balance in our life and it's very important when you walk out that door to leave it at work, and then to focus on the other important things in your life.

#2; not buy into other people's emotions, specifically I mean guilt. Because very easily there is a sense of guilt laid upon the clinician by the general public, be it on purpose or otherwise. I like to remind new graduates that we didn't tell the client to get a pet. We didn't make the pet sick. Often, we may feel guilty because we can't magically fix this patient quickly, within a budget that suits the client.

#3; to not keep things in. You've got to reach out for help. If in doubt, reach out and ask. Be it your mentors at work, colleagues, people from your cohort, someone that you did some internship work experience with perhaps.

? **DIEDERIK:** If you were starting again, would you be a vet?

... **GARY:** Absolutely I would. I love the profession. I love the sense of contribution to the community, the team that I work with, the work that I do. I would absolutely do it. We're privileged to be able to do what we do.

? **DIEDERIK:** You've had some major challenges. What were two or three that you faced?

... **GARY:** The biggest challenge was a situation ten or so years ago, we were expanding rapidly, we were about to build a new hospital and we had offered equity partnership to two associates. They chose to open their own practice about a kilometre down the road. They opened their doors right as the excavators moved in and started demolishing our site. That was the most challenging experience on a range of levels.

The positive out of that was that I feel so resilient now that it wouldn't matter what happened, it's all insignificant relatively speaking. That had quite an impact on our business, but we survived and I find myself in the situation I'm in now where I couldn't be happier.

The second one would be raising a young family whilst working long hours, and being deeply committed financially to a new business. I think that's a very tricky scenario to negotiate. To successfully manage a lifetime relationship, be it in marriage or otherwise, but to be able to be there for your life partner and keep everything afloat at the same time, that was tough.

The final thing personally was when we took on the business. Because we're in a regional area, there was no support with after hours, we were pretty much on call 24/7 for several years, and that was incredibly taxing.

DIEDERIK: Balancing family, career and fatherhood, how did you and Pricilla make that work?

GARY: It was by identifying the best ways to grow the business and to put in additional human resources that would free us up to start living our lives without a hundred percent commitment to the business. The order was to build the business financially, build it in terms of the resources by way of the people in there, and that would then allow us to step back.

DIEDERIK: What does success look like to you?

GARY: Success is living life on your terms. Doing the work that you're passionate about, doing it when you want to do it, doing the work that you want to do, having the time to spend on everything else in life that's important to you and having the financial results to give you the freedom to do all those things.

DIEDERIK: What were the keys to those successes?

GARY: Finding the most effective ways to make the practice financially successful, and that was learning how to develop very slick systems for marketing and for managing the client experience. Then separately to that, learning how to lead, so that it wasn't just me pushing this thing on my own, it was in fact 20 people doing it together; all highly engaged, highly aligned, highly motivated and treating it like it was their own business.

DIEDERIK: You're always motivated, up, focused, how do you manage that?

GARY: I'm highly-disciplined. I'm a true believer that our most precious resource is our own energy, more so than time. Because if you've got time, and you have no energy, then the time is effectively wasted.

So, I look after myself first, I keep myself fit, I'm very wary about my diet. I meditate. I spend time in the morning preparing for each day to recalibrate and prepare, it can be incredibly powerful. I have continued a dedicated journey of personal development.

I do a lot of reading and self-education. And I implement. That's a self-fulfilling prophecy; the more you implement, the more success you enjoy, and success breeds success. The more you extend yourself outside your comfort zone, the bigger that comfort zone gets. That development becomes addictive.

NOTE: You can find the remainder of this interview online at:

www.VeterinarySuccessSecretsRevealed.com

Key Take-Aways

- What they didn't teach us at University is that you spend much more time working with people (your clients and your team) than you do with animals and we were never prepared for that

- Do not buy into other people's emotions, specifically guilt. Because there is very easily a sense of guilt laid upon the clinician by the general public, be it on purpose or otherwise

- Get comfortable with the notion that you're in sales. Because whether you like it or not, you are selling a diagnosis, a diagnostic plan, you're selling yourself and you're selling the practice

- Don't keep things in. You've got to reach out for help

- Success is living life on your terms, doing the work that you're passionate about, doing it when you want to do it, doing the work that you want to do, having the time to spend on everything else in life that's important and having the financial results to give you the freedom to do all those things

> "Is owning a pussy-cat or a puppy-dog a right or a privilege? Yes – it's a privilege. So then how about having people working for you, a right or a privilege? Yes – again a privilege. So, if it's a privilege to have people working for you – are you then rewarding them with your gift of leadership?"
>
> Diederik Gelderman

Dr Geoff Golovsky

Dr Geoff Golovsky

BVSc(hons), MANZCVS(SAS)

> *"There is nothing in which the birds differ more from man than the way in which they can build and yet leave a landscape as it was before."*
>
> ~ Robert Lynd

Geoff graduated from Sydney University in 1998. He spent a year down the south coast of NSW, a year in Thailand working for AUSAID and then at Post Graduate Foundation in Veterinary Science. Subsequently he spent almost three years working for multiple employers in London.

On return from London, Geoff worked at North Shore Veterinary Specialist Centre where gained his memberships in small animal surgery.

In 2006, he started his own practice in Double Bay (Sydney). That practice is now a successful five-and-half vet small animal practice that provides all the services his clients are after.

He is an active member of the AVA and has been on the committee of the AVAPM and scientific committee of the AVA. He organises the Australian Veterinary Sailing team and part organises the AVA sailing. He is also on the organising committee of the Practice Insight tours.

In his spare time, he is a life-saver at Bronte Beach, a keen sailor – and a keen stand-up paddle surfer. He also attempts to be the best husband and father of three amazing kids who are eight, five and three.

DIEDERIK: Geoff, what ignited your passion to be a vet? And at what age did that start?

GEOFF: I don't remember wanting to be anything else. I went through the policeman and fireman stage, and then I was going to be a vet, from about seven or eight, it's all I ever wanted to do.

DIEDERIK: What didn't they teach you at vet school that now that you look back, you think, *"Hey, they should have taught us this?"*

GEOFF: Unfortunately, vet school is all about learning your science and anatomy, and it completely forgets the fact that vets must be communicators. If you can't communicate with your clients, you will not be a successful veterinarian.

DIEDERIK: Where did you learn to communicate?

GEOFF: I don't know. I think I've always been able to talk to people. The school that I went to had a very, very broad focus. It wasn't academic, in terms of it was encouraging you to do drama and to do sport and do teamwork. My father said to my kids the other night, the best thing that you can do as a child to go and work in retail, so you can learn to communicate.

I don't know where I learnt it. I was scrubbing boats as a kid, but it was something that just came innately to me to be able to communicate with everyone on their terms.

DIEDERIK: What did they teach you at Uni that has proven to be incorrect in the cold hard light of veterinary practice?

GEOFF: They don't teach you communication and they teach you that it's all about being a scientist, I think it's not an education.

It's about communication, and you're never going to be able to do surgery if you can't convince the client to like you, respect you and trust you.

DIEDERIK: If we had a new graduate sitting in today, what are three things that you'd suggest that they do immediately to turbocharge their career?

GEOFF: Anyone who can get into vet school can do the science and stuff. But they must be open to be taught. They need to learn communication. Go and do an acting course or a toastmaster's course, or just get out into the public. They need to be able to find someone who can communicate, and they need to be able to watch them and learn practical skills. They need to just go and talk to people. Get out, stop reading your textbooks and get out into the public somehow.

DIEDERIK: What are two or three things that that same new graduate immediately needs to stop doing to ensure their career is going places?

GEOFF: The lecturers used to say that we were Australia's finest, the best and the most intelligent. And I think vets come out with a bit of an *"I'm awesome,"* and they need to get back to reality.

They need to stop thinking that they are the best thing since sliced bread, and they need to stop. Gen-Y, they're just the pits in terms of thinking that put a smiley face at the end of something and it's suddenly okay. They need to start to be professional, and need to start to realise that they must work hard and it just doesn't lay out easily.

There's a lot of people in our profession now who want to work two or three days a week, and they don't want to do after-hours because it's too hard. I remember the days when we did 80-, 90-hour weeks. There was no award to look after them. Obviously, we all adhere to the award today, I adhere to the award as well but it doesn't mean you don't have to work hard at the times that you are on shift. Keep answering the phones, lunch is sort of put into your mouth at some point in between the rest of the day. If they want an office job, there's plenty of office jobs out there. Being a veterinarian is not a 9–5er. It's not a sit down and have lunch business. They've got to get out and experience what practice is all about.

DIEDERIK: If you were starting over again, would you enter the same career path?

GEOFF: I did GAMSAT exams to get into Medicine several years ago, and I was this close to not being a veterinarian, because the stark reality of the job was very, very different to what I thought it was going to be. I did all my work experience in veterinary practices, as a kid, it was everything that I ever wanted, and it was a big shock to the system once I got into practice.

I love what I do now. I love every day, but I have oscillated over the last 18 years of my profession. I'll keep a yes/no.

DIEDERIK: What were three major challenges that you faced?

GEOFF: The harsh reality of the job, the hours and the expectations threw me.

My first job was not a very good job, and I struggled. I think now, with communication. Being in touch with mentors and friends, I think probably made it a bit easier, because everyone goes through the same thing. But, I felt very much alone, number one.

When it came to getting to the point of buying my own business, I got screwed twice by respectable colleagues. I worked out that business and friends is a very, different thing. Money is very different. I found that a real lesson. I learned a lot from that.

Starting my own business from scratch, it's the hardest thing I ever did, and I don't think I'd ever do it again. I'll never do it again by myself. When it comes to working seven days a week, 15 hours a day, trying to maintain a relationship, it's just ridiculously difficult.

DIEDERIK: So, how did you manage to balance family, career, fatherhood? Obviously from what you're saying at certain stages there, it was difficult, maybe even impossible?

GEOFF: An incredibly wonderful wife. We've got three kids now. At one point, we had two nannies to get through the day. Between my wife and I, she was working full-time, I was working full-time, we'd have to drop the kids to school. One nanny would pick them up, one would be at home with the baby. It was a disaster, and I think our kids suffered from it. I think now, I'm lucky that my wife has decided not to work.

Unfortunately, one of my veterinary mates just got divorced. Our job is not a 9–5 job, and we need partners who understand it, or we need to be able to have a safety net...whether it'd be nannies or whatever we have to pay. And something that I've learned is that your relationship you have work on it. Like your business, you must work on your relationships constantly. The number of holidays that I spent writing on my computer trying to catch up with my notes and doing work and not spending time with the kids. You need to talk about it. I do know now that if the kids are around, I don't work. If I'm at home, my computer is off, which means I do get more behind, but these are the things you have to do.

DIEDERIK: I see you as one of the successful young practitioners. What does success look like to you?

GEOFF: For me, success; if my kids can experience the same upbringing, because I was lucky in my upbringing, if they can experience the same thing, then I've been successful.

So, it's not a business goal.

DIEDERIK: What have been your biggest successes and what have been the keys to those successes?

GEOFF: I've only been able to achieve what I've been able to achieve because of work.

The success of building VetHQ to the level that it is now, we'll celebrate our ten-year birthday in a couple of months' time – we are now a five-and-half vet full time practice, with six-and-half vets on the team, and a total team of 30. And I started wondering whether or not I should employ one nurse or two nurses when we started ten years ago.

I never wanted to open up another veterinary hospital because I'm taking away and I'm competing with my neighbours, and there are neighbours within kilometres of each other. But, I've done it differently and I've become bigger than almost all my competitors, purely by listening to my clients and understanding what they require, tailoring what they think they need and what their pets need to make sure that they understand that.

And so, if it comes, the biggest success is having two ears and one mouth. Listening twice as much as you talk, and communicating appropriately to make people respect you, like you and want to come back to you.

DIEDERIK: You're always up and motivated and focused. What have you found to be the best ways to keep you like that?

GEOFF: In the last five years, I've taken up stand-up paddle surfing, and that's the only thing that's kept me sane. I used to sail a lot. But sailing takes three to four hours in and out. I don't have time anymore. Water has always been important to me. So, in waves and being absolutely hammered and within an hour, you can do strength exercise and get that bit of water that I need.

Right now, it's the only thing that's kept me sane. It has kept me going, and even on a bad day, I could be down at the beach at 6 am and have a little bit of a play.

Exercise is really important. I would probably do yoga as well. I started doing a bit of yoga, but time...I've asked my yoga teacher whether she will do it at nine o'clock at night, because that's about the time that I get out that I get to stop, and of course she won't do that.

> **DIEDERIK:** What do you think holds back most practitioners from achieving what they want to?

NOTE: You can find Geoff's answer to this question and the remainder of this interview online at:

www.VeterinarySuccessSecretsRevealed.com

Key Take-Aways

- Keep exercising, keep fit, get some regular down time, meditate and relax
- Communication is THE key to having a successful career
- You are not alone
- If you want to succeed, then you need to work hard
- Develop a support network of family, colleagues and mentors

> "So many practice owners building their lives around their business when they really should be building their business around their lives."
>
> Diederik Gelderman

Dr Glen Kolenc

Dr Glen Kolenc

BVSc (Hons)

> *"The greatness of a nation and its moral progress can be judged by the way its animals are treated."*
>
> ~ Mahatma Gandhi

Following receipt of his BVSc (Hons) from Sydney University in 1997, Glen instantly moved to Griffith, NSW and worked for 18 months. He then returned to Sydney where more opportunity for surgery was available. After three years, Glen was exhausted and disenchanted, overworked and run down. He considered following the required path to become a surgical specialist but chose the alternative option of moving overseas.

Glen spent the next four years in the UK, working as a locum. He loved the lifestyle. Living it up like this is what made Glen realise that there is much more to life than work.

Returning to Sydney in 2005, Glen soon started to feel those same old feelings that came with long work hours, weekends, public holidays and after-hours' work. The opportunity to purchase his own veterinary business arose and he took the plunge. After three years, he had never felt more snowed under.

After attending some business management courses, he shifted his mindset from viewing the clinic as a vet hospital, to seeing it as a business. Since then, he has been building his business to work for him.

In 2013, Glen started a love affair with French Bulldogs. Word got out that there was a vet that breeds Frenchies and before too long Glen had a loyal following of French Bulldogs coming to his clinic. Going against the traditional grain of the way vets see themselves, Glen started marketing himself as a French Bulldog enthusiast under the alias Dr Frenchie. He now has over 300 French bulldog patients, a number that is rapidly growing.

DIEDERIK: Glen, when did you decided to become a vet and why?

GLEN: At school, I had no idea what I wanted to do, but I was a science geek, I was interested in the medical side of things, and there was something in me that I wanted to do something that was valued.

I didn't want to be a lab dude; I didn't want to be a researcher. Considering those thoughts, veterinary science was the first thing that came to mind.

DIEDERIK: Glen's in a very particular niche – can you explain when you went into this and why?

GLEN: In 2012, my wife announced that she wants to get a French Bulldog, and breed. We're talking about 15 years from graduation.

I worked for ten years, had my own business for about five years by then. When we had our first litter, I just fell in love with the pups. I was absolutely smitten by the whole experience. I'd never been into breeding before, I hated breeder clients.

When we had our second litter, I started to discover Facebook and a few different French Bulldog groups; networks of people that sold puppies. People were putting all sorts of questions; from the questions and the answers, I could see that in the vet world, the breeding world and the pet owning world, that French Bulldogs were a very misunderstood breed.

I just started to answer people's questions and put comments in to help them out. I was giving big long detailed answers, in several different groups around the country. Soon, when someone put a question up about their French Bulldog, people were tagging me, and say, *"Hey, this guy Glen seems to be helpful."* And I was doing that day in day out, because I was a bit of a Facebook addict. I was probably answering up to five to six people a day, and that soon doubled. Then one day, someone said, *"I should come meet you instead of you helping me on Facebook. I'll just come and see you,"* and I was flattered, because I was just doing it with the will to help. Then the next week, someone else came in, and then next week someone else came in. Then the next week, one of the people that had come in started recommending me on Facebook. *"Don't bother wasting your time getting help from people here. Just go see Glen. He was really nice. He helped me a lot."*

That was mid-2014, I just checked and now we have about 250 French Bulldogs on our records. And, I've got a really big reputation.

? DIEDERIK: What do they call you now?

... GLEN: I'm Dr Frenchie. That all happened in a very short time. Then I started a Facebook page and a blog called Dr Frenchie.

French Bulldogs are a breed that have a lot of unique issues that all happen to be in the areas that I was not skilled in (dermatology, airway surgery, etc.). I couldn't do airway surgery, I hated skin. But I've been seeing so many of them and building up this reputation and calling myself Dr Frenchie, I just had to master them, as much as I hated them.

So, I went and learned dermatology properly, and I learned how to do airway surgery.

? DIEDERIK: You've got people coming from all over the state and inter-state? And it all started because you were generous with your time.

... GLEN: Yeah. After work, when I had done everything I had to, had dinner and put the kids to bed, I'd be there answering questions.

I did that all from a place of pure pleasure, I wanted to help, there was no ulterior motive...There was never *"If I do this, hopefully people start bringing their dogs to me."*

People will even put comments on Facebook, *"This Glen, he must be genuine because I've seen him give really long helpful answers to someone in Melbourne, so obviously he's not doing it for the money..."* I've even answered emails from people overseas to help them.

That gave me so much pleasure knowing that these French Bulldogs are now fixed up.

DIEDERIK: What things, did they teach you at University that you now know are just not true in the real world?

GLEN: My thought is, not so much they taught me something that was incorrect, I just don't think they taught us properly about what the real world was going to be.

DIEDERIK: What didn't teach you at University that they should have taught you?

GLEN: They didn't teach us how to be a vet in the city of small business.

They taught us how to be a vet in the city of specialist clinic where generally, by the time people get referred there, they know they're up for a big bill, and by then, money is generally never an issue, they just do whatever they say. That's not how it works in the real word.

DIEDERIK: If you were talking to a new graduate, what are the three things that s/he should do immediately to turbocharge their career?

GLEN: They should get a job in a busy clinic to learn all the basic skills, the basic day in day out stuff. Don't focus on the complicated cases.

Next, would be to learn business basics. If you can, do that part-time in your first couple of years. Get yourself set and then as soon as you can, get your own clinic and hire 'guns'. Hire a fantastic team; make yourself the dumbest, most useless technical person in the business.

DIEDERIK: The other side to that question. What are the three things they've got to avoid in their first couple of years if they want to get themselves firing?

GLEN: Avoid working in a quiet clinic, or in a clinic where the boss doesn't let you explore a bit. Avoid focusing only on improving your vet skills, also learn business skills.

Learn the basics of being a good vet and of business. Book into a business course, rather than advanced medicine.

DIEDERIK: If you were starting again, would you, in fact, still be a vet?

GLEN: For most my career, I would have said *"No"*. Now that I have found my passion...now, that I am in my passion, if I could do it again, I would. I'd also be thinking outside the box earlier.

DIEDERIK: You sort of fell into this niche, but someone who's frustrated can ask themselves – *"What am I passionate about and go looking for something?"*

The next question is what three or two big challenges have you had?

GLEN: One challenge that I had at the start, was realising that I'm not good at the problems that I was going to be seeing. How the heck could I stand there and say that I'm this French Bulldog guru when I'm not good at stuff? So, I did have the fear that I might not be that technically good vet, able to manage 'it'.

Another was with the Veterinary Practitioner's Board. I need to be careful, I can't call myself a French Bulldog specialist or a French Bulldog expert – so I call myself an 'enthusiast'.

That was a 'little' fear. But the 'big' fear was just from other vets, especially from the local vets who were wondering why I was getting so many of their French Bulldog clients.

DIEDERIK: How do people watching overcome those challenges?

GLEN: The VPB – by being very careful with my language and wording – I'm NOT a specialist. I am a breed enthusiast.

The other two, what other vets are saying about me, and fear of not being a technically good vet. Honestly, feeling that I couldn't do the best job for the breed that I wanted to do the best job for. Made me feel like I couldn't hold to my vision.

So, I just mentally thought; Right, I've got to learn the skills. I have to just face it like a raging bull and learn how to do...

DIEDERIK: You've got a family, so how do you balance fatherhood, career, and business and family?

GLEN: Sometimes it's a struggle, but generally, I guess, one of the blessings is having your own business. When our kids were younger, I took a significant amount of time off work. I would just get relief vets so I could be there for those early, important days; growing up, lying in bed with them, do whatever.

I preferred to not put the money in my pocket. I wanted to be there...I just made the choice.

I don't know if I achieved a good balance, but I had a very valuable experience. I did in fact take excessive time off, and then eventually, you realise you have to actually have money. So, then I spent time working a lot more, but I still made sure I had quality time at least.

The bigger picture, I think for me, was the fact that I owned the business, I had that choice to take time out and see the kids. If I was an employee, then I could not do it...

DIEDERIK: If one of your kids said, *"Dad I want to be a vet,"* what are the three or four pieces of advice that you're going to give him or her?

GLEN: Similar to what I'd advise a new graduate; work in a busy clinic, get your basic skills, learn about business, buy your own clinic, learn marketing and leadership, and be healthy.

DIEDERIK: Paint us picture of success.

GLEN: Here's a business sense answer; having a profitable clinic that runs on autopilot, but the key part of that is with me working in the business only because I want to.

DIEDERIK: What have been your biggest successes in life or business?

GLEN: In business, building up over 250 French Bulldog clients coming from everywhere in two and a bit years.

DIEDERIK: What are the keys to these successes, and I think we already been through that. And I think passion is probably the most important one.

GLEN: Getting into this niche, it's the first time I've ever had an... *"I want to get out of bed to go to work"* level of passion.

DIEDERIK: The first time in seven or eight years now.

GLEN: Nineteen years.

I've always thoroughly enjoyed being a vet, but for most of my career, I've always been thinking about what else would I do. There was never anything anchoring me deeply to vet. The trouble is I didn't know what I wanted to do.

DIEDERIK: What for you is the best way to stay focused and motivated?

GLEN: The big thing is changing to a healthy lifestyle. That keeps me more focused and motivated than you could imagine. We've both turned into health buffs (eating, exercise, meditation), that keeps me focused more than I thought it would.

DIEDERIK: If you had the chance to do it all again, what, if anything, would you do differently?

GLEN: I'd buy a business sooner.

DIEDERIK: What do you think holds most vets back from achieving their goals?

GLEN: Conforming to the norms of their profession, and a fear of getting 'found out'.

DIEDERIK: Do you think either tragedy or luck, has played any part in your success?

NOTE: You can find Glen's answer to this question and the remainder of this interview online at:

www.VeterinarySuccessSecretsRevealed.com

Key Take-Aways

- Overcome and master your fears and challenges
- I hated being a vet, until I found my dream niche, my passion
- Vet is my job, but it's not me
- Get good at the basics of being a veterinarian and at the basics of business
- Decide that you want to, are going to be successful

> "Vets live in the 'grey' zone – where you're not making enough profit to be happy, but you're not so badly off where you're broke. This means you can bitch and moan without really having to take action and do something about it."
>
> Diederik Gelderman

Dr Glen Richards

Dr Glen Richards

BVSc

> *"Until one has loved an animal a part of one's soul remains unawakened."* ~ Anatole France

Growing up on a grazing property in NW Qld is where Glen's love and passion for animals began.

Glen graduated from the University of Queensland (1988) and worked in multiple practices in Australia and the UK before buying a small vet practice in Townsville. Within ten years, he had developed five vet clinics and a pet store in Townsville as well as two veterinary hospitals in China. From there, he went on to build an integrated pet care empire, which now operates more than 160 veterinary hospitals.

Glen is the founding Managing Director of Greencross and was a co-founder and Director of Mammoth Pet Holdings (Petbarn).

Since moving from an executive role, Glen spends his time as a professional investor, mentor, and company director. He is on the board of: Greencross, 1300Smiles and Regeneus. He is actively involved with Monserrat Day Hospitals, SmartClinics medical centres, and myFootDr podiatry clinics.

Glen continues to help foster early stage businesses through mentoring, investing and strategic planning sessions. He regularly does public appearances and speaking engagements to share his scaling up story and V4P message.

A devoted family man, Glen is married with three daughters, and still lives in Queensland.

DIEDERIK: Glen, what ignited your passion to become a vet and at what age did that happen?

GLEN: I grew up on a sheep and cattle station and I thought I was going to be an accountant. My dad said, *"What are you going to do when you finish grade 12?"* I said, *"I'm going to do accounting."* He said, *"Why would you want to do that?"* And I said, *"What do you mean?"* He said, *"Why don't you do something useful?"* I said, *"What do you mean?"* He said, *"Why don't you do veterinary science? That'll be useful if you decided to come back on the land or you might be able to go elsewhere for it."* And I said, *"You know what dad? That's actually quite right."* My dad put me up to it.

Was I really passionate? I was eager to be involved in the profession, but I don't think I was obsessionally passionate about it.

DIEDERIK: You went into an alternate-type career path and ended up with Greencross. What led you on that journey?

GLEN: I always had a very strong interest in business. I always had this concept of keeping an eye on revenue and expenses and always chatted about it at the kitchen table. I was about to head back from London to Australia and rang up a practice in Townsville and said, *"I'm interested in buying a practice. Are you interested in selling me your little branch practice?"* I got enough info to say, *"You know what, I would like to buy the main and the branch. Don't tell anyone else they're on the market, and I'll be back in three months and we can finalise the negotiations and the deal."* And that's exactly what happened.

I got on a train in Moscow to travel back to Australia – the Trans-Siberian Express, and wrote a business plan for a vet practice in Townsville. By the time I got to the end of that seven-day journey, I had written a business plan for a network of veterinary hospitals across Australia called Greencross.

I always had that business plan, and it wasn't until I met up with some other like-minded vets, about seven or eight years into owning my own practice, that we started putting together this idea of a network of hospitals.

I remember being quite frustrated about this concept, I couldn't get any traction until I met John Odlum and Keith Knight and we started meeting regularly and built the model.

It was just an evolution, but you've got to seize the opportunities.

DIEDERIK: What didn't they teach you at vet school that you now know is important to being a successful vet?

GLEN: We needed a much stronger business backbone. As a graduate, you want to be competent clinically, but it can be done within a framework of being business ready, and I don't think any graduates are business ready or aware. We graduate incredibly naïve on a whole range of things.

Basic business awareness and communication skills are vital. And they marry up nicely to the fact that whether you're in research or whether you get your own practice, having some of those basic business skills is vital.

DIEDERIK: What did they teach you at vet school that you now know is just incorrect or was a waste of time?

GLEN: It's a diverse profession and we have to cover stuff that we never use again. It's what they call a BVSc, bloody versatile science degree. It gives a pretty good grounding in life on a general sense. There are not enough people in the veterinary education system that are reasonable business people as well as being great clinicians. You're allowed to be both.

You've got to be able to put food on the table. There's a lot of frustration because graduates come out on a very low salary and they never work out how in their career path to 'have it all', be great clinicians and to have a fulfilled life and by the way, having wealth will be fine as well.

DIEDERIK: What are three things that a new graduate must do straight off the bat to get career ready?

GLEN: First; do not accept a job where they get hung up on the location – get hung up on your first experience instead. Look for a great mentor, within the profession or outside, who is going to be your sounding board as you make big career decisions; where you're going to practice, what you're going to practice in, or are going to do a PhD or whatever.

Battening down your clinical capability is vital. You've got one to two years of simply having to lock down all that theory and that little bit of practical experience that you got through your undergraduate years.

Become competent quickly. You arrive as a not-quite-work ready graduate, and you've got a couple of years of going through an 'apprenticeship', to be work ready and competent, and then you can lift your head.

While you're building those clinical capabilities, you have to learn the business side of life. You've got to put some time into reading and up-skilling yourself to make yourself more capable in the business world.

DIEDERIK: Is there anything that you believe they need to avoid doing?

GLEN: Young graduates are still the same. Their first year in practice, they burn themselves. They'll spend 12 hours a day at the clinic, go home and keep reading, and so they end up pretty tired, frazzled and they'll bump in to a few cases that'll absolutely rock them so that they're quite distressed or frustrated that they're not quite as knowledgeable as they thought they were. So, have a good mentor to slow you down a little.

DIEDERIK: If you were starting again, would you in fact be a vet?

GLEN: I have really enjoyed the profession. It's given back a lot. I know I've put a lot into it. I'd probably do it all over again because working as a clinician, working as part of a community or a companion animal vet, where you are part of a community is just a wonderful feeling.

DIEDERIK: What were two or three major challenges you faced?

GLEN: The biggest one...you're in a community of other vets, how jealous they could become of your success.

I was prepared to work longer, harder and smarter than my competitors, but my competitors wanted me to treat them as more important than my clients. It bewildered me.

DIEDERIK: How did you manage to balance your family, your career and fatherhood?

GLEN: If you spoke to my wife, I'm pretty sure she'd reinforce that we didn't balance it too well.

It's a tough one because when you are working the long hours of a companion animal practice, getting there at 7 am, getting out of it about 9 o'clock at night. As you walk in at night, my wife is keeping our little babies up just so I could actually see them.

Through the hard years, there wasn't a lot of balance. It was all vet work, and then on my days off, it was all family. And even when we listed Greencross, I said, Monday to Friday, I'll do whatever it takes for the company, Saturday and Sunday is family time.

Family time is vital, but what you miss out when you play that game is you miss out on time for yourself...

During my years as CEO, Monday to Friday, for the company, Saturday and Sunday is for the family. And I made that a very strong point that through that period we always had proper holidays with the family. Even while I was a companion animal vet, we'd lock out and block out our holidays a year in advance so that we had proper holidays together.

DIEDERIK: What does success look like to Glen Richards?

GLEN: I'm big on the balance of being healthy, good relationships with the family and friends, time for community, time for physical and mental health. But, look, at the end of the day, success is all in your own goals. One of my goals was to be able to be retired by fifty. I resigned from Greencross three months before my fiftieth. That enabled me to spend to spend a lot more time with my kids; more time for my family and more time for me.

DIEDERIK: What are your biggest successes, and what were the keys to them?

GLEN: On a business part, taking a little vet practice in Townsville to be an ASX 200 company and having shareholders who were exceptionally happy with the performance of the company; moving the culture from mediocre to a culture of success so that our employees were exceptionally happy; and having clients who were exceptionally happy. We achieved a lot as Greencross.

On the family front; to have your family around you, not having gone through a divorce; having a healthy and positive relationship with my wife and my kids is vital to who I am.

On the health part, getting reasonably healthy and trying to exercise at least four times a week.

DIEDERIK: You're always motivated and focused, how do you stay that way?

GLEN: The important one is having inspiring people around you – peer mentors.

The other one is having reflection time. I go for an eight to ten kilometre run pretty regularly, I'm always jogging and thinking and turning things over in my mind, so that helps balance things up and weigh things up.

And of course, having my wife who is a good sounding board, who I would be able to bounce things off, and my dad when he was alive being one of those mentors.

DIEDERIK: If you had the chance to do it all again, what would you do differently, if anything?

GLEN: The number one thing, if I had to look at the business side, the veterinary side, Greencross, I wish we hadn't listed in 2007. Either we should have spent a lot longer unlisted and just quietly went about our business, way out of the sight of the investment community.

DIEDERIK: What do you think holds most vets back from achieving their goals?

GLEN: It is one profession that doesn't lift their vision high enough. For some reason, we don't value ourselves as a profession. We think perhaps we're poor cousins of the medical world, we've got to lift our vision and start thinking a bit bigger and, by doing that, we achieve a lot more and challenge ourselves a lot more.

? DIEDERIK: Do you think that luck or tragedy has played any part in you achieving your success? Or, was it just hard work?

GLEN: I still remember Trevor Farmer who said, *"LUCK, labouring under correct knowledge."* I've never forgotten it.

When you are putting passion and time and effort in the right direction, you create your own luck. I love the phrase, *"The more I practise, the luckier I get".* And it's exactly that, it's just hard work. You work out that big, hairy, audacious goal that you're trying to achieve, and then it becomes easy because once you know where you want to head, then you create all those little steps in between to get there. Most of us, unfortunately, never work out what that big, hairy, audacious goal is. It's usually pretty small, and they stay inside their comfort zone and they don't stand right out there on the edge, because it hurts. And most of us who are successful put ourselves out on the edge, and it hurts.

? DIEDERIK: If you were helping someone else, what are some pitfalls are you going to tell them to avoid?

GLEN: I would keep reminding them that at some point they're going to burn out because it is a profession that is quite emotionally fatiguing so they've got to manage themselves. They've got to have good friends and family around them. They've got to have mentors they can bounce off when they're having those bad days, just someone just to bounce off and reposition them.

It is a profession that fatigues people. Every interaction you have; you are conscientiously giving a little bit of yourself in every interaction. So, it's little wonder that over time, you do burn out. You've got to repair yourself weekly, if not daily. You've got to repair yourself annually through your holiday patterns and pulling back from the brink.

DIEDERIK: What is your passion?

GLEN: I can make it easy by saying my family is my passion, and everything I do is simply to create a better world for me and my family. To some degree, that's true, but at the same time, for the purpose of this interview, my passion...I look for problems and I get excited by the problems I see and find. So, for me, having done 'prac' work and worked with a whole host of middle-aged vets that hated being vets, I realised I had to work out how to try and solve that.

My passion is, I guess, scaling up businesses and tackling industry problems that seem big.

DIEDERIK: Our industry has a reputation, what do you think has kept you sane?

GLEN: Friends and family and holidays. To some degree, I think it's having that outside influence and the ability to have a timeout. That repair time is what keeps me sane.

When people tell me they've not had a holiday for three years, I'm just mystified because everyone gets a holiday, can take time out. Whether it's simply sitting at the beach, enjoying a surf or going bush-walking. We live in Australia, we're so lucky that here is so much around us that's free and accessible, so no one has got an excuse for not having repair time and cleansing themselves.

DIEDERIK: You've already talked about a number of things that you've given back to the community. What else have you given back.

GLEN: Right now, I'm big on mentoring. I have a number of young business people that I mentor with at least five hours a week going into mentoring young business people to try and achieve their goals and support them.

My wife and I set up our own foundation and we have five different charities that we support.

DIEDERIK: What do you consider to be two or three keys or attributes to success?

GLEN: Planning, vision, and people. Because at the end of the day, to really achieve, you have to assemble a team, and you have to put time, effort and energy into culture and time, effort and energy into supporting your people. And once you realise that you don't have to know everything, you simply have to find or form a good team, be it in a veterinary practice or be it in a big corporation. Once you realise you don't have to be the hero, you have to be the person that supports everyone else around you, it becomes much easier. Hold them accountable, give them the responsibility for the job you want them to do and be there to support them.

DIEDERIK: Was there ever a snap point, a turning point, a defining moment or a line in the sand?

GLEN: Opportunities just keep rolling past your front door. And you will know when you're game enough to leap out through that door and jump on one of those opportunities. There are a number of really important points in my life (both personally and professionally) at which that has happened.

It's about taking a risk, and the worst that can happen is someone says *"No"*. And once you realise that it's okay when someone says no, you feel pretty bad about yourself, but, geez, if you don't get out there on that edge, that edge that says *"I'm going to have an exceptional life, I'm NOT going to have an average life,"* then you're not going to get to 90 and die with no regrets.

? DIEDERIK: Last question. What's your vision for the future of the veterinary industry?

⋯ GLEN: It's a fabulous profession. The pet has moved from the backyard into the bedroom, so we are well positioned as a trusted adviser to the community and to families across the western world. Our job is to take that seriously and we do that through making sure we have facilities, equipment, larger teams, and hospitals that are able to deal with proper full-service veterinary care. Be it boutique veterinary hospitals or be it corporate practice, it doesn't matter, our job as a profession is to meet the expectations of society and that is to look after a pet that is positioned as a family member.

We will continue to grow our practices; we'll continue to use new communication tools. We need to continue to skill up our profession so that we meet the expectations of people that now treat their pet like a human so we need to have human grade and human like capability at our vet hospitals, and we need to skill our people up to match that expectation.

DIEDERIK: That's an awesome place to finish. Glen, thank you very much for all your fantastic information.

Key Take-Aways

- For some reason, we don't value ourselves as a profession
- It is a profession that fatigues people. With every interaction you have, you give a little bit of yourself 'away'. So, it's little wonder that over time, you burn out, so you've got to repair yourself weekly, if not daily
- As a new graduate, you want to be clinically competent, but at the same time, it can be a done within a framework of being business ready

- The profession suffers from a position of not valuing themselves enough and lifting their vision enough and not seeing where they could get to.

- Most of us who are successful put ourselves out on the edge, and it hurts out there and that's why so many won't do it

> **"The most insidious disease in our profession is that of low self-esteem and poor self-worth. This needs to change"**
>
> Diederik Gelderman

Dr Isabelle Resch

Dr Isabelle Resch

BVSc(Hons), MVS, MANZCVS (SA Medicine)

> *"All of the animals except for man know that the principle business of life is to enjoy it."* ~ Samuel Butler

Isabelle graduated from the University of Sydney in 1991. She worked both in Canberra and Sydney in small animal practices for ten years.

She gained her Masters of Veterinary Studies (Murdoch University) in 2001 and sat membership examinations in Small Animal Medicine in 2001.

She purchased Inner South Veterinary Centre (Canberra) in 2002 in partnership with three other veterinarians. The practice was subsequently rebadged, revamped and renovated to become the Inner South Veterinary Centre that you see today.

In 2010, the owners started on a journey of progressive practice management and on practice management continuing education. This process allowed the practice to grow and prosper and in Isabelle's words, *"Ramped the business up to another level".*

Isabelle continues to work at ISVC – which is now a six full-time equivalent vet practice with a staff of over thirty.

Isabelle passed her membership examination in veterinary behaviour in 2016.

She has two boys (seven and eight), and successfully juggles kids, veterinary practice ownership, marriage, study and work. All of this she says is a still ongoing challenge!

DIEDERIK: What ignited your passion to become a vet Isabelle, and at what age did that start?

ISABELLE: I was passionate about becoming a vet from about 12 years old.

It was a slightly bizarre choice. My parents don't like animals. There's no family history of vets, animals, doctors, nothing, and I just had decided I wanted to be a vet and kept on pursuing that passion.

DIEDERIK: What didn't they teach you at University that is important?

ISABELLE: They didn't teach us about resilience. To be a veterinary professional in today's world you need to be resilient. The other thing is you need to find that motivation within yourself. You can't always look to others to spoon feed you the answers to the difficult questions.

DIEDERIK: What did they teach you that turned out to be untrue?

ISABELLE: There is a big emphasis on technical skills, knowing everything about Cushing's disease, diabetes, etc. That's not what gets you through your career. There are far more important skills; client skills, rapport building skills, getting on with the people around you, the people you work with. University did not prepare us well in that way.

DIEDERIK: If we had a new graduate sitting across the table from us, what are three things they must do to turbocharge their career?

ISABELLE: They need to learn how to connect with people. They need to realise that being a vet is dealing with people because no animal comes in without a person attached to them. They need to be able to deal with the people within the practice as well.

When you start developing good relationships, it takes money out of the equation. Your clients believe what you say and listen to only what you say. When you have a good rapport with the client, you can use that wealth of knowledge that you've got.

DIEDERIK: What are three or four things that a new graduate should avoid doing to make their career takes off?

ISABELLE: The three things are; avoid inertia, the *"I'm sure it's too hard"* mentality. Avoid being *"I'm too busy, I'm too stressed, I'm too tired to..."* and you go on and on. Those first few years, they're amazing years, good years. They're the hardest few years. For me, it was definitely the hardest years of my life, but they were also, retrospectively some of the most rewarding. You need to avoid saying, *"I'm so tired, I'm so busy. I'm stressed."* You need to keep on getting out there and utilising the resources that are there, the people that are there, and just don't sink in to being *"It's too hard. I'm not good enough"*. You need to motivate yourself and avoid inertia.

DIEDERIK: Would you choose to be a vet again, retrospectively?

ISABELLE: If I knew everything that I know now and where I'd end up, yes. I think yes is the simple answer.

DIEDERIK: What were two or three major challenges that you faced?

ISABELLE: The biggest thing is practice ownership and your work–life balance. Not working too hard, making sure you have time for your family and friends, the passions that you have in life that are non-vet.

Finding the right partnership. You need to be on the same page, you need to have the same work ethic, you need to be driving in the same direction, and that is not always easy to find.

DIEDERIK: How did you manage to balance family, career and motherhood?

ISABELLE: With difficulty at times. I have a very, very supportive, and understanding husband, who picks up a lot of my pieces.

I also outsource. I have a cleaner, I have a gardener, and I have a nanny who helps me. You need to prioritise, and I've certainly had to prioritise the little things.

It's been a struggle sometimes to balance it, but I think you need to have it balanced towards your family. The other thing we did from the very first day at Inner South Veterinary Centre was, we decided that work–life balance was a priority, and we put in place certain guidelines that would be our priority. We only work eight-hour shifts; we don't do the twelve-hour shifts. We don't do after-hours. We're closed on Sundays. We rotate regularly through weekends. We just make sure that we're not working too hard. And for the other mothers at work, or for everyone in the practice who needs to...they can work half the time.

DIEDERIK: That's good, start with the end in mind when you started the practice so you built your practice around your life and not your life around your practice.

ISABELLE: It's not always been that balanced. We have gone through a few ups and downs when the practice took a bigger chunk of my life than I would like it too. But there are other times where I would walk away for four weeks, go away on holidays, and my business partner looks after the place and I can walk away happily.

DIEDERIK: In vet, as a woman, do you face more challenges than the guys?

ISABELLE: There are quite a lot of unconscious biases here, but I also think that some of the vets finding it harder make it so themselves to a degree. I think they're not always ready to ignite themselves as much and sort of just go, *"I can't do this. I've got too many balls to juggle."*

I also feel that as a woman, sometimes, you tend to always sort of be looking at *"God, I need to be doing this, and I haven't done that very well,"* as opposed to sometimes thinking *"Okay. Well, look at what we have achieved. Let's celebrate what we've actually done."* And I think, the obvious, the finding the balance between kids.

DIEDERIK: You're one of the new breed of successful practice owners. What is success to you?

ISABELLE: Success to me is personal.

It's not about dollars, it's not about degrees, it's not about letters behind my name. Success is about feeling fulfilled as a person and as a professional. Feeling that I've developed, grown as a vet, as a mother, as a wife, as a colleague, as a business partner, as everything.

DIEDERIK: What have been the keys to making those successes happen for you?

ISABELLE: Some of the biggest keys have been getting mentors in my life. It's probably going back to the earlier question, *"What would you say to a new graduate?"* Getting a mentor, and then changing mentors over. As you develop and as you grow in different directions, you need different mentors.

Continuing education is one of the most important professional development tools, but that doesn't necessarily have to mean going to conferences all the time. It can be going to workshops, it's talking to people and not just vets. I think we need to look far more broadly outside of that little paradigm...We're not just talking to or about vet schools, I'm talking about the life schools. And going outside of the profession, going to things about leadership, business management, personal development. I think that's really helped me. The goal is to keep on moving, the goal is... not stopping, you need to keep on moving.

DIEDERIK: You're always up and motivated and focused. What's kept you like that?

ISABELLE: You need to look after your physical and mental health. I exercise a lot, I eat very well, I try and get regular sleep. I tried to take timeout, sometimes I too would go *"Yeah...well, let's have some time with the family."* I take really long holidays. I have lots of interests outside of work. I'm a passionate skier, so I make sure I really do spend time doing the things I love and especially non-work related. Because when I spend the weekend skiing, I'm recharged. Life is a new slate again.

DIEDERIK: If you were doing it again, what would you do differently?

ISABELLE: It's very heavy...The retrospect scope is a cracked thing where you look back and you look back and you go, *"What do I change?"* I don't want to change a lot. I enjoyed the journey, it's an ongoing journey, it's still got lots of challenges.

DIEDERIK: A lot of vets don't achieve their goals, and they certainly don't achieve what you've achieved. What do you think holds most of those people back?

ISABELLE: Self-doubt. *"I can't do it. I'm not good enough. I don't have the skills."* And inertia. *"I couldn't quite evolve many of my skills,"* or *"I couldn't quite..."* You can lead a horse to water and all that...

DIEDERIK: Has luck or tragedy had any part in what you've achieved.

ISABELLE: The simple answer is, *"I was just chatting to my butcher this morning, and had a little bit of chat about 'gosh, I've been lucky.'"* And he said, *"Actually, you know it's not about luck, it's about what we've done with our lives."*

So, I would actually say no. You don't let the circumstance dictate where you end up, you decide where you want to be and move towards it.

DIEDERIK: What pitfalls are there that someone who wants to be successful should avoid?

NOTE: You can find Isabelle's answer to this question and the remainder of this interview online at:

www.VeterinarySuccessSecretsRevealed.com

Key Take-Aways

- You won't be spoon-fed the answers – you need to go looking yourself
- Communication and 'getting on with other people' skills are equally if not more important than technical skills
- Avoid the *"I'm too busy, I'm too stressed, I'm not good enough, I'm too tired to…"* mentality
- Build your practice around your life and not your life around your practice
- Look at what we have achieved. Let's celebrate what we've actually done

> **"Concentrate on the core aspects of your business that can never be taken away from you, consulting, diagnosing, prescribing, imaging and surgery."**
>
> Diederik Gelderman

Dr James Ramsden

Dr Diederik Gelderman

Dr James Ramsden

BVSc

> *"Cows are amongst the gentlest of breathing creatures; none show more passionate tenderness to their young when deprived of them; and, in short, I am not ashamed to profess a deep love for these quiet creatures."* ~ Thomas de Quincey

James graduated from the University of Melbourne in 1991. He's worked in small animal, mixed and equine practice around the world from Melbourne to Lexington, Kentucky.

In 2001, he founded PetPack – providing online marketing products to vet clinics – a business with four guiding principles:

- Teach people about how to look after their animals better
- Reinforce the role of the vet as the leader in animal health care
- Highlight the impact of animals on human happiness
- Make a useful connection between pets and a healthier planet

This interest in marketing stemmed from an interest in talking to people. As a young vet, it quickly became clear that the conversation was stopping when the client left the clinic – leading to poor outcomes that could be prevented.

James brings extensive media experience to the business allowing PetPack to deliver the effective communications. James's experience includes ten years with the *Australian Women's Weekly*, six years with *Good Morning Australia* and regular appearances on *Today*, *Weekend Sunrise* and 3AW.

DIEDERIK: What ignited your passion to become a vet James, and at what age did that start?

JAMES: Originally, I wanted to be an airforce pilot, and I didn't pursue that because my eyesight wasn't 100%, and in those days, you needed 100%. We had pets, and my grandfather was a beef farmer. So, there's a real interest in animals. My grandfather was an early conservationist and he used to spend hours taking us out to see birds and things like that.

DIEDERIK: You've gone into an alternative route. Can you just quickly precis your career?

JAMES: One of the first things I did in practice was to call my clients. This was early on. I graduated in the early 90s. Ultimately, I just like talking to people. In my view (of veterinarians), generally you're either into the technical side, which is like carpentry or getting the job done. Or, you like the front-end part, which is where you're connecting with the clients. For me, it's the front end. I've done a lot surgery but I find it stressful. Whereas with people, I've been in some very difficult situations with people and it's not always fun, but I quite enjoy that challenge of making the connection.

I started ringing clients. When I graduated, no one rang clients. When I say, I rang clients, I was ringing them to see how the animals were. The second person I rang said, *"I paid the bloody bill, what are you ringing me for?"* In those days, mostly the only time they ever got a call was when their account was overdue.

Quickly I worked out that it was really productive to ring someone 48 hours later or three days later because you could head problems off at the pass, and the clients loved it. They couldn't believe they're getting the call.

From there, I started thinking about other things that you could do, and we build a little email tool that I used myself, and then I started selling that to other vets, and it was quite organic really. A few things came along, like the internet was invented. But, all the way along, I've maintained that interest in communicating from the vet to the pet owner, and as a result, PetPack today provides services that help vets communicate directly with their clients, or get new clients coming in.

DIEDERIK: What didn't they teach you at vet school that you know now you should have been taught?

JAMES: The people at Uni were academics, they didn't have a lot of commercial experience of any type.

There was no education around the importance of communication and for me, in vet practice communication makes all the difference. It could be as simple as giving people the space and time to make decisions around expenditure. But, probably more significant, or of greater impact, is that role that we play in helping people understand the choices they can make. My view is that the pet owners that we're dealing with, generally want to look after their animals well. The reason they don't is it's too hard. It's either too hard because you've got to remember to do something every month, or it's too hard because the problem's hidden and the expert hasn't made it clear to you that the problem's there, and then help you make that decision.

DIEDERIK: New graduate...what are two or three things that they need to do immediately to turbocharge their career?

JAMES: The most important thing would be to get one foot into the commercial world (practice or industry) early on. The issue with that though is that when you're at University, you're not that interested in what's going to happen next.

And to follow your passion when you can, and sometimes, it's not obvious.

University can be very dry, because they've got a lot of material to get through, and it doesn't often go outside the borders of the straight up and down veterinary stuff. So, as much as possible, keep your passion alive by exploring how you can get that to work.

DIEDERIK: Same new graduate, what are two or three things you're going to tell them they've got to avoid if they want to be successful?

JAMES: Give up. It's going to be difficult following the pathway of being a vet. There's a range of challenges and there's going to be points where you are going to want to stop. Don't just stop and walk away, but have a think about whether or not that's the right decision. Because it's okay to walk away. If that passion is still there, I would encourage you to keep going and you'll find a way around that. Just keep going because you have confidence in yourself to find that pathway.

DIEDERIK: If you were starting out again, would you in fact be a vet?

JAMES: Absolutely. Veterinary science is the best training you'll get. Because you can converse with anyone across those topics and have a sense of what's going on quickly.

DIEDERIK: What were two or three major challenges that you faced?

JAMES: I worked with a guy who I didn't get along well with. That was difficult. I was pretty young and I started a new practice with another bloke, which was great at the start but when decisions needed to be made about the direction we were going, it became clear that we weren't going to be working together.

Another one was whether or not to continue practicing or develop the online business that lead to PetPack. It might seem easy in hindsight now when we got a thriving business that we could say that that was pretty straightforward. But, to actually get off the pathway from traditional veterinary practice is difficult.

Thirdly was surviving in a new business where you've got cash-flow issues. I'm happy that I've been through those because I've learned a lot and it changed the way I operate, but they weren't necessarily pleasant.

DIEDERIK: How did you balance your career, family and fatherhood?

JAMES: From the start, I felt, so did my wife, that it was important to spend time with our kids. I grew up like a lot of my generation where my father wasn't around a lot. One of the advantages of owning your own business is, you have the capacity to be flexible with time. In the early days, cash was pretty tight so there wasn't a lot of room to move but, the value of being there when my boys were little was amazing.

DIEDERIK: What does success look like to you?

JAMES: It's a range of things. It all comes down to me feeling like I've reached my potential.

Then, there's more long-term things where you look back on a project. It's all about asking yourself that question, *"Are you up, or going for your potential?"* and then, *"Are you actually going to do it?"* And then doing it.

DIEDERIK: What are the keys to success in general?

JAMES: It's having a balance. Understanding what the key priorities are. Business is important, family is important, community is important and the other one is my own personal development and health. As much as I can, I put effort into all those areas.

Another part of success is having a partner that you trust, a life partner, because it's easy to get off track. So, it's very good working with someone else in your life who can say, *"Look, just put your head up for a sec and have a look"*...it doesn't have to be one person, but in my case, one person has been fantastic.

DIEDERIK: You're always up, focused and motivated, how do you stay that way?

JAMES: I certainly spent a lot of my career double-guessing or worrying about whether I'm doing the right thing. So, I work pretty hard on maintaining a positive and even view.

A couple of things have been instrumental for me, but most importantly – mindfulness. I came across a guy called Craig Hassed – a GP who taught the Monash Med students this back in the 90s. I had a bit of anxiety, or I had a tendency towards anxiety, and mindfulness is a good way to manage that. That's an important part of it because that allows me to reduce the amount of chatter going on my head, and chatter is excessively detrimental in my case.

The other part of it is when I get in front of people, I'm much more in the moment, because that's my natural place to be. I enjoy being in a public setting or having a chat.

DIEDERIK: If you had the chance to do it all again, would you do anything differently?

JAMES: I would, from an early age, practice mindfulness. Looking back, I had very little control of what was going on in my head.

The other thing is I would have liked to engage more in the real world as opposed to the academic world or the school world, so I had a better commercial sense of what's going on. Because my commercial sense is an area that really needs to be improved. We're a lot better commercially in our business than we were when we started.

DIEDERIK: What holds most vets back from achieving their goals?

JAMES: They don't ask. As a group, they're not inclined to ask the question. They might have an idea of doing something but they won't go and ask someone about it. They assume it's not going to be possible.

Also, the mindset of the veterinary business model is limiting and it's also under pressure for various reasons. Most vets are not making the time to go outside of the business and think... Sit on top of a mountain for instance, and spend time thinking about what's going on.

DIEDERIK: Has luck or tragedy played any part in you achieving your success?

NOTE: You can find James' answer to this question and the remainder of this interview online at:

www.VeterinarySuccessSecretsRevealed.com

Key Take-Aways

- Good quality communication, for me, in vet practice makes all the difference
- The pet owners that we're dealing with, generally want to look after their animals well. The reason they don't look after them is it's just too hard
- Following the pathway of being a vet is very difficult and you've got to make a conscious decision to follow it through and not to give up
- To get off the pathway from traditional veterinary practice is pretty difficult if you're talking to your colleagues about that because most people look at you sideways and go *"What the hell are you doing? Why would you do that?"* You need to remember to do what's right for you
- The mindset of the veterinary business model is limiting, it's also under pressure for various reasons, and it's difficult to get out of that mindset. Make the time to get out of the business, sit on a mountain top and think

> **"You always have to proceed with insufficient knowledge – that's the difference between someone who makes something happen and the procrastinator who doesn't."**
>
> Diederik Gelderman

Dr James Tiernan

Dr James Tiernan

BVSc, GPCert(SAM)

> *"A dog is the only thing on earth that loves you more than you love yourself."* ~ Josh Billings

James was raised in country Queensland. Becoming a veterinarian was a dream which started in primary school.

Following graduation from the University of Queensland in 2001 James moved to the UK and worked in several busy small animal clinics. Whilst in the UK, James successfully passed examinations in a General Practitioner Certificate in Small Animal Medicine [GPCert (SAM)].

After spending eight years in the UK, James and Jane (his wife, also a veterinarian) returned to Australia. James spent a short period working at the University of Queensland Veterinary Small Animal Hospital before moving to Victoria and working at the Western Animal Emergency Centre, Werribee in 2009.

In 2010 James and Jane purchased Highton Veterinary Clinic (Geelong) with a team of nine staff. The clinic now a team of 26 team members.

Since purchasing HVC, James and Jane have managed to have four young children. James loves being a business owner, a veterinarian, and becoming a father to Seamus, Niamh, Aislin and Declan, as well as all their pets.

DIEDERIK: James, what ignited your passion to be a vet? And from what age did you make that decision?

JAMES: I always had aspired to be a vet from a quite a young age. I grew up in country Queensland. We lived in a small town, so I was exposed, as young child to lots of small animals. As a child, I had goldfish, birds, cats, dogs, the 'usual' types of pets. And I always loved caring for them, liked being involved with them. It's just general, I guess, a love for the pets and stuff like that. I always had passion for the animals, and I think I always had a caring, nurturing disposition for pets.

DIEDERIK: Thanks. Here is an interesting question; what didn't they teach you at vet school that you know retrospectively is vital to your success as a practicing veterinarian? And, where can someone else learn that?

JAMES: I think for a lot people at vet school, they teach you how to (whether it's in a systematised way or in a very 'thinking' way) get a diagnosis. But I think for a lot of people, it's the case of how they bond with the client that should be more important. If they don't have a relationship with the client, the client loses trust with them and the result is that the client then won't believe and won't trust you to do a procedure. And I think most vets know what procedure to do in order to get them to, the answer. The challenge is how to communicate along the way.

So, I think it's really communication skills at that level; to be able to explain 'stuff' to the client. Your job is actually dealing with the public, it's actually not just hugging puppies and kittens. I think a lot of people go through vet school with the assumption of holding and cuddling puppies and kittens. So, when they get out in the real world – and we found this with people we've employed – that they didn't realise the amount of client exposure they would be exposed to, which then causes them frustration because it's way out of their comfort zone.

? DIEDERIK: What did they teach you at vet school which retrospectively turned out to be totally incorrect in the real world of veterinary medicine?

JAMES: I think vet school for me was quite good. Fortunately, I had some good lecturers. And particularly when I got to my clinical years, I think some of their attitudes were very strong with their regard to customer focus; maybe some possibly less so. They probably, didn't emphasise the importance of, the business perspective of a practice. My vets are employed in a business setting, they know that we're running a business, we're working in a business and working for a business, and the finances are attached to it. So, I think a lot of times, that was explained or wasn't stressed to be as important, and when you move down the track, you realise that's just wasn't covered as much.

? DIEDERIK: Talking about new graduates now; what are the three things that a new graduate must do as soon as possible or immediately, to turbocharge their career?

JAMES: I think a lot of times they don't realise how much time they've got to spend developing themselves as people. And, whether that's...I guess, myself as new graduate, when I sort of didn't know something, I asked one of the other vets about it. I also did 'it' on my own. I had to study at night-time or later to follow up on cases so I hope I knew what to do next time. I'm very much hands-on, so I guess for me, it was the case of getting my hands in it and doing the procedure, and perhaps sometimes – not fumbling, necessarily, but getting my way through and then perhaps reviewing it afterwards to see if there were other ways of doing it. But I think a lot of it's getting your hands in and being involved, which I think a lot of vets stand back at the start as new graduates, and kind a want to be – they want to be maybe shown it in a different way, or bits and pieces. I think it's a case of getting yourself out there and being exposed as much as you can.

I think sometimes it's also a case of pushing the envelope, pushing as such that perhaps you're outside your comfort zone, it rattles your cage, that's where you learn faster rather than being more passive and hoping to learn by reading a textbook. At University, you learned everything, but those go-getters, that perhaps may not have been the most academic at University, but they're most hands-on with the bits and pieces in practice and in finding the cases. I think you develop faster that way.

DIEDERIK: And the other side of that coin, what are the three things that you need to avoid doing to turbocharge your career?

JAMES: I think being down about themselves, the pessimistic attitude. I think overwhelming with stuff with the stress of the job, and at the end of the day, you've got to enjoy it. You're in here to do it for the next period of your life. I think it's a case of making sure you enjoy it. So not getting wound up, bogged down in the days, I guess…whether it'd be in 'sadness', for lack of a better term. But I think it's a case of not getting overwhelmed and bogged down and losing your enjoyment of it.

I think the more you get overwhelmed, it becomes more and more of a struggle; *"poor me, it's so hard,"* and not asking for help perhaps. Or *"I'm too proud for ask for help".*

DIEDERIK: If you were starting all over again, would you be a vet?

JAMES: Yeah. Totally. I love it.

DIEDERIK: You've had challenges – name three big ones.

JAMES: I think…I guess from a family perspective, like at ten years of age, I had some family tragedies. My mother was diagnosed with breast cancer, my father died very suddenly. My younger brothers and I just had to move on, and mum's quite strong. I think I get that determination from mum. So, we just had to get up and keep going with it. So, I think that definitely made me quite determined not to be knocked back in bits and pieces. That, in effect, getting in to vet school, made me actually more determined to get into vet school despite the way things unfolded. And so, I actually did a degree first, and then finished that degree and went into vet school afterwards as it were.

As a business, we've had ups and down from staff dramas; whether it'd be staff leaving, going and coming, or not agreeing with our way, the way we would like to run our dream practice, to many other challenges along the way.

DIEDERIK: I see you as a really successful veterinarian. One of the modern young breed, if I could use that term. From your perspective, what is success? Paint us a picture.

JAMES: I guess success for me, is having a very supportive wife; having four gorgeous kids, which...we love them and they love us. Having family time when we can. From the financial side of things, having a well-oiled clinic machine that produces an income that satisfies a lifestyle which Jane and I aspire to or are comfortable in. That we're not having to stress over certain things. I think it's case of then...also the dream is down the track, having a situation where Jane and I can retire comfortably with a lifestyle that we would be comfortable with. So, I guess that's the dream. I think we're well on the way to that.

I think it's supporting the team as well. So, having a really well-functioning, hard-performing team. That they'll enjoy their job and they enjoy coming to work, because I think it makes my life easier and Jane's life easier, as owners and vets working with their team that want to come to work.

We have a very supportive practice manager who definitely supports us completely from a business side of things. And so, then I guess it's having support from others, whether it'd be extended family or people like yourself who can help guide you along the way.

DIEDERIK: There are a lot of vets out there that don't achieve what you've achieved, and don't achieve what they want to achieve. Any idea what holds most of them down?

JAMES: A lot of them are thinking *"It's too hard"*. It's like putting it into the 'too-hard basket'. Or *"Poor me, I can't do that"*. Or *"The client won't want to do it..."* They instil their disbeliefs; I guess – for lack of better word – but perhaps they perceive their client as not wanting to do what they want their client to do. If you ask the client, they'd probably want to do the best thing for their pet. I guess it's how they find out that there are ways out of that negativity. They think they're getting negative clients. They are unable to help the pets either. They're not even enjoying their job. They're not enjoying medicine for the pet. So, I think it's a case of pushing the envelope. If a client won't pay and you don't charge, it has a negative effect on everything.

DIEDERIK: If someone came up to you and said, *"James, can you mentor me? Help me."* What couple of pitfalls would you say, *"You've got to avoid this?"*

NOTE: You can find James' answer to this question and the remainder of this interview online at:

www.VeterinarySuccessSecretsRevealed.com

Key Take-Aways

- Ask if you don't know. People are generous with their time and will help you out
- Develop a supportive environment or network of people with the same goals and aspirations that you have
- Set goals, write them down, they're your light at the end of the tunnel
- Don't be afraid of what other people think
- Hang around with people who excel at what you are striving for
- Every animal comes with an owner

> **"The most common reason why Veterinarians don't achieve their goals, practice and life ambitions...They don't REALLY believe that they deserve it."**
>
> Diederik Gelderman

Dr Judy Harbison

Dr Judy Harbison

BVSc, MBA

> *"The greatest pleasure of a dog is that you may make a fool of yourself with him and not only will he not scold you, but he will make a fool of himself, too."* ~ Samuel Butler

Judy is the principal of and has owned Bulimba Veterinary Surgery since September 1994. She has grown the practice from a one-person clinic, to be the multi-vet, purpose designed clinic hospital that it is today.

She graduated from the University of Queensland in 1990. Now that Judy is busy with a family of three small children her clinical hours are only part-time but she maintains regular contact with her clients and their pets. Her particular veterinary interest is surgery.

She shares her home with a Burmese cat named Flower. Judy is a Director of a not-for-profit organisation 9CVLC, which operates a desexing and microchipping clinic at the Logan Pound. Judy is passionate about continuing education, and completed an MBA in 2013.

Judy is a Director of Judhar Pty Ltd., which owns seven small animal practices in Brisbane. Her clinical work is ongoing, combined with the ever-expanding task of practice management.

Her three children are central to her non-work life and she remains passionate about the veterinary industry, and is also interested in the interface between veterinarians and other care professionals.

DIEDERIK: So Judy, what ignited your passion to become a vet and at what age did that occur?

JUDY: I had the blessed upbringing of having a father as a vet with a clinic under our house in Central Queensland. At probably, eight- or ten-year age bracket, it would have become a full-blown conclusion that I would be the vet in the family.

DIEDERIK: What didn't they teach you at vet school that you know now to be absolutely crucial in the real world of veterinary science?

JUDY: Clearly, business skills were not taught in any way. We had professional studies where we did one or two lectures; I probably would have done that a bit earlier. Also, pursuing the collegial aspect of the veterinary profession, that's something fairly unique to our profession that we should celebrate and exploit.

DIEDERIK: You get new graduates passing through your practices. If one was sitting here with us now, what would you suggest they do immediately to turbocharge their career?

JUDY: Seek out mentors, both clinical and, if they're interested in the business side, find some solid mentors.

Immerse themselves in as much hands-on practice as they can, and in the early stages of their career, that should be clinical and it should be varied. I would get a broad experience. Large animal practice lends itself to having to learn on.

Then thirdly to find your area of interest. You're going to immerse yourself in a 40- or 50-year career, so try to find your niche within that.

DIEDERIK: The other side of that coin, same new graduate, what would you suggest to them that they need to avoid doing?

JUDY: Avoid professional isolation. So, putting yourself in a one-man practice in a branch practice where you don't have any colleagues or mentors would be suicide in my mind.

Also, making sure you're learning from people who are doing best practice. Don't put yourself in a scenario where it's near enough is good enough or you just cut corners. And have a look at industries outside of vet, and learn communications skills. Don't put yourself in a scenario where you just run to the back of the building and say, *"I don't do people,"* because it's clearly not that profession.

DIEDERIK: If you were starting again, would you, in fact, be a vet?

JUDY: Absolutely. I would probably overlay that with some business skills which I've done myself through an MBA, and if I was starting over, I would bring that in earlier.

DIEDERIK: What were two or three major challenges that you faced in your career?

JUDY: Understanding cash-flow, not realising that money in was not always money to the bottom line. In the early days, there were a few moments where it was nail-biting close to not being able to pay wages or bills.

And then, a major challenge is HR, mostly around managing poor performance and knowing and when to exit the toxic elements that seem to infiltrate at times.

DIEDERIK: How did you balance family, motherhood and your veterinary career?

JUDY: So, that's an ongoing challenge. I've got three children, so I'm living the dream right now. I start my day early and make time for my children in the afternoon and evening. That's just passion that works for our family. The challenge of trying to have it all is exhausting at times.

DIEDERIK: What does success look like to you?

JUDY: For me, it's about freedom of choice. I don't want to be told that I can do this and I can't do that. I want to have my choice with time, choice with my money, choice with my activity. So, success for me is freedom of choice.

DIEDERIK: What have been your biggest successes, either personally or professional, and the keys to those successes?

JUDY: What gives me pride is the balance of family and business. So, whilst it's a big challenge, it's also one of those high priorities.

I think my biggest success is being clear about what you're happy to compromise on, being clear on your priorities and not shifting from that, and the key to it, is just being dogged about it. For me, children are first and then business, even though business occupies my every day, it's all to the extent of my family, having a family that's well balanced.

And it's a hand brake sometimes, particularly for women, that you will not compromise your family but at the same time, if that's your priority, then that must be the first decision that other things revolve around.

DIEDERIK: You're always a motivated, focused person. How do you stay like that?

JUDY: I read a lot. I talk to colleagues. I'm passionate about what we do. I live and breathe it. I think I'm fortunate to have found a profession I love and have found avenues in it that are still fascinating.

DIEDERIK: So, you don't have to work a single day in your life as it were.

JUDY: Absolutely. Sometimes — but when employees are clocking off and counting hours and looking it's 38 hours, I actually feel freedom around that because I don't have that restriction. If I want to work Sunday morning at 5 am or Thursday night at 10 pm, that's actually my choice. Nobody is telling me to do that, and I don't have to do that. So, I don't have any envy of people that are locked in to a 38-hour-week.

DIEDERIK: If you had the chance to do it all again, what would you do differently?

JUDY: I would probably take learnings from other industries. I think sometimes, in vet, we can be a bit narrow-focused. It's a very small industry, but there's a lot of similarities to other allied health professions, and even human health profession. We shouldn't restrict ourselves to just thinking we have to learn within the veterinary space.

DIEDERIK: You've achieved a lot of goals, and there are so many practitioners out there that don't achieve many at all. What do you think holds them back?

JUDY: Fear of change. Fear of failure. Definitely on the clinical level, there's a fear of failure. Many, particularly new grads, will not have an attempt to do a surgery, whereas, fortunately, when I graduated in the 90s, we were able to. We weren't given the fear of litigation that probably a lot of them live with now.

And, in the business sense, vets/owners, not understanding leverage, so how to make best use of money, and particularly, other people's money and particularly, the banks' money. Understanding that took me a while.

DIEDERIK: Do you think that tragedy or luck has played any part in you achieving your goals?

NOTE: You can find Judy's answer to this question and the remainder of this interview online at:

www.VeterinarySuccessSecretsRevealed.com

Key Take-Aways

- It's a 40- or 50-year career – find your area of interest and expertise
- The challenge of trying to have it all is exhausting at times but, it's absolutely worth it
- I think sometimes, in vet, we can be a bit narrow-focused. It's a very small industry, but there's a lot of similarities with other allied health professions, and even human health profession, we can learn from them
- I don't want to be told that I can do this and I can't do that. I want choice with my time, my money, my activity. So, success to me is freedom of choice
- 'Luck', is around a result of consistent effort, and taking advantage of opportunities when they present.

> "A veterinary practice seeking long term success can no longer compete based solely on the products and services that it delivers on their own. A practice must be able to define and communicate and live by and for an underlying purpose. Only then will long term success ensue."
>
> Diederik Gelderman

Dr Kim Kendall

Dr Kim Kendall

BVSc (University of Sydney), MACVSc in Cat Medicine, Examiner in Cat Medicine,
MACVSc in Animal Behaviour

> *"Thousands of years ago, cats were worshipped as gods. Cats have never forgotten this."* ~ Anonymous

Dr Kim Kendall, cat vet, has been messing around with cats' minds since last century. She has worked and travelled extensively both in the UK and the USA.

A 1982 graduate, she narrowed her focus in 1990 with an MANZCVS (Cat Medicine), and then broadened it again in 2004 with an MANZCVS in animal behaviour. She worked with the (Sydney) Cat Protection Society in the early 1990's, and was the first to routinely spay and castrate kittens at seven to ten weeks of age.

She is a world expert in feline friendly care, one of only two cat-only vets in Sydney and the only cat vet in Australia qualified in cat behaviour. She continues with the calm pursuit of excellence in Feline Medicine and Feline Health, both mental and physical! She is mindful that we humans have changed cats' environment – from solo desert-dwelling rodent hunter to City Gods and Goddesses. Kim also delivers regular seminars and webinars and has been presenting seminar papers on feline behaviour and medicine topics nationally and internationally.

? DIEDERIK: Kim – what ignited your passion to become a vet, and at what age?

... KIM: It happened when I was about seven, and I started saying that I was either going to be vet, a teacher or air hostess.

DIEDERIK: You went into what I call an 'Alternative Career Path', a feline and behaviour path. Why, when and how did you do that?

KIM: I actually wanted to be a goat vet. I always had a view of where I wanted to go. I wanted to be an elephant vet, but I wanted to be an elephant vet in Balmain (Sydney), and I couldn't make that business plan work. I decided, I liked goats, so John and I moved to England because I figured that the intensive care of sheep there was very close to goat practice in Australia.

In 1985, I realised that cats were underrepresented; a sick cat was a dead cat. Then I started to try and find out what was really going on with the cats. There was a practice based in Bristol called the Feline Advisory Bureau, and they had interns there who knew about cats. So, I used to call them up and find out about cats. The more you know the better. The other people in my practice would send me the cats, and so you get to know more and more about less and less basically.

I heard about feline only practices in America, so I went to work in America and learned more. In 1992, John and I drove a 1966 Buick from Cape Cod to L.A. and visited a lot of feline practices on the way.

During that trip, the East Chatswood Cat Clinic was born. So, in 1994, we set that up.

DIEDERIK: What didn't they teach you at vet school that retrospectively, you know is crucial to your success as a veterinarian?

KIM: What they didn't tell me was that every animal came attached to an owner, including wildlife, the government owns wildlife. The other thing I learned in Zimbabwe was the robustness of the organism; I think we forget that now. If you just push the animal a little bit along the way to health, they can take over and get better. If you're working with the animal to get better with, say, with things like trauma or diseases that we have drugs for, then you only have to push them on their way and they will work with you.

Unfortunately, we also see the situation when you're working against the animal. And that seems like cancer and many new diseases. And then the push is really up hill.

DIEDERIK: What they did teach you at vet school, which in the real world of veterinary practice is incorrect?

KIM: They taught us to chase the zebras instead of to look for the horses and look after the horses well.

DIEDERIK: I understand.

KIM: It took a long time...before I wasn't looking for Cushing's disease in every dog and cats that were drinking too much.

You have to handle a thousand normal animals in order to understand what normal is, from each of the species, and that's difficult.

If you understand that it's going to take time until you can be excellent once you've graduated, I subscribe to the 10,000 hours of excellence theory. If that was promoted a bit more, it would take off the pressure, then you could think about your errors and your successes as part of the learning process, part of the acquisition of something that can't be downloaded. No one can teach you excellence. That's a motor skill and a mental skill.

DIEDERIK: Based on your experience, again, what are the three things that a new graduate must do immediately to turbocharge their veterinary career?

KIM: Understanding how the nurses are trying to help you. They'll cover for you or support you and you're going to feel a lot better about what you're doing then. You can put them off-side and make them feel unwelcome and inadequate, when really, the vet nurses' going to be so more experienced than you in just the mechanics.

So, learning to get the nurses on side, and it might only take chocolate cake.

A lot of practices are now doing dentals. So, I think you probably must know your way around teeth and a dental machine.

I don't know if you can have it before you graduate—but what I've discovered is animals don't read the textbooks, so are you going to have to understand that the first few animals you see haven't read the textbooks and they're not going to present with 'classic symptoms'. So, you're going to have to be in there asking…So, if you understood what you didn't know, you could ask for help.

DIEDERIK: What were three major challenges that you faced in your career?

KIM: I've always had too many options. It would have been nice to have a narrower path, because choice can confuse you and consume your productivity: *"Should I do this? Should I do that?"* In fact, you eventually have to decide on what you're going to do and go for it, and where you have to put your energy. It's alright to be defocused for a couple of years, but you really do need to decide on a path and go for it.

DIEDERIK: If you had a son or a daughter, and they were about to start on a veterinary career, what are some things will you advise them?

KIM: Spend a year as a vet nurse, in a decent practice. Do the two-year vet tech degree, work as a vet nurse and earn some money, get some more experience, and then go to vet school.

You have to get the 1,000 hours' experience and if you're a vet nurse, you are not responsible for them. There's a huge difference between being able to help them and being responsible for the outcome.

DIEDERIK: What does success look like to you?

KIM: Success, to me and to a lot of CEOs of big companies, is about work–life balance. I work 100% of the time. What's balance? I enjoy my job. However, in order to sustain relationships and so forth, you need time away.

Success to me is not finding the vet work too challenging. I reckon that accepting and doing 85% of your vet work really well, that's success on the professional part, and it should lead to success on a business part, and, if you can blend that with however much social life you need...

So, success to me...we sat down and wrote a business plan for our lives. People write business plans for their businesses, but when you're a microbusiness, that's going to include your partner and kids, etc. We decided what kind of unit we wanted to live in, what kind of car we wanted to drive, and I decided that I wanted to ride horses on my days off.

DIEDERIK: What have you found are the best strategies for keeping yourself focused and motivated.

KIM: Continuing education. I have an insatiable curiosity. And, I'm really disappointed these days that so much is now down to opinion instead of fact. Why is it so? Who said it was so?

DIEDERIK: If you have the chance to do it all again, would you do anything differently? And, what would you do differently if you do?

KIM: What I'd do differently is understand and address the process of depression in vets. I thought it was me that was the problem, but it's not. It's a chemical imbalance, and it's set up by the way we approach the things that are out of our control.

If I had understood this better as I approached 40; and I think for women 40 is an important point. I know quite a few female vets who wanted to get out of vet practice at about 40, and I don't think it's coincidence.

DIEDERIK: What do you think holds most vets back from achieving their goals?

KIM: I think Sam Bowden has a point. Vets are actually afraid of success, because if you're successful, then for some reason – being successful seems to be the antithesis of what vets want to be. I think if you understand that we are tradespeople, we are tradespeople in the companion animal arena, and most of what we do; we are supporting someone else's passion.

If you make most of the animals that you see, comfortable in tradesman like fashion; there's good tradesmen and bad tradesmen. And, take the pressure off perfection and the disappointment of not being able to do more, I think you can create a balanced perspective for yourself and a better life for pets.

Think global and act local. I do the best that I can for the animals under my care, and I can make a difference to the community, then that's going to be more emotionally and mentally stabilising for me.

DIEDERIK: You have a perspective on the business side of the practice versus the clinical side of practice. When did you make that differentiation?

NOTE: You can find Kim's answer to this question and the remainder of this interview online at:

www.VeterinarySuccessSecretsRevealed.com

Key Take-Aways

- Get focused and go for it
- Write down your goals and keep referring to them
- We are just tradespeople
- Don't expect all pet owners to be as passionate about their pet as you are
- Ask for help
- Trust and verify

> "Building better self-esteem and self-worth needs to be part of the undergraduate curriculum at Vet school, because without these skills, most veterinarians never achieve their true potential."
>
> Diederik Gelderman

Dr Mark Ethell

Dr Mark Ethell

BVSc, DACVS

> *"And God took a handful of southerly wind, blew His breath over it and created the horse."* ~ Bedouin Legend

Mark graduated from the University of Sydney in 1990 then entered mixed practice in Orange NSW for a year before returning to do a Master's degree and Large Animal Residency at Camden. More advanced training beckoned and he completed a Residency in Equine Surgery at the University of Florida leading to becoming a registered specialist and Diplomate of the American College of Veterinary Surgeons in 2000. As Senior Lecturer in Surgery, Mark practiced and taught at Massey University in New Zealand for three years before moving back to Australia to join Canberra Veterinary Hospital as a partner in 2002. Mark led the expansion from one practice to five over the next ten years before consolidating his practice interests in Canberra Veterinary Hospital and Canberra Equine Hospital in 2013.

Mark is a specialist horse surgeon, Managing Director of the Canberra Veterinary Group of practices, co-founder of VetShare Limited, as well as Independent Vets of Australia.

Mark was the Founding President of the Australian Veterinary Business Association and has served as President of the Australian Veterinary Association (ACT Division), Honorary Fellow of the University of Melbourne Veterinary Faculty as well as a member of the University of Sydney Steering Committee for their Veterinary Teaching Hospital. Mark is also a Member of the Australia and New Zealand College of Veterinary Scientists by examination in Equine Surgery as well as a Fellow of the Australasian College of Biomedical Scientists.

Mark's mission is to help more companion animals lead longer, happier and healthier lives both with his own hands as well as by helping to facilitate the success of other vets and their practices. When not at work, Mark loves spending time with his wife, four children and beloved pets.

DIEDERIK: What ignited your passion to become a vet Mark, and at what age?

MARK: I was 12. We were always into pets because my family had a farm on the Central Coast of NSW. I just loved that whole mix of being able to combine a career in science, but also going to the great outdoors and with the animals that I loved, and the interaction with people.

DIEDERIK: You had a different career path to the 'normal' vet. Can you explain what you did and why?

MARK: I found a routine path into rural mixed practice the country town of Orange (NSW). I quickly learned that there is great skill and knowledge that you need. So, I thought that the secret was to specialise more and more in a narrower field. I happened to love surgery and I loved horses. So, I went back to Sydney University where I became a specialist in Equine surgery.

DIEDERIK: Then?

MARK: I loved being an academic. I loved teaching, loved research, and loved doing the surgery. But, I looked at my colleagues and I could see that it was a long path to get ahead. I had four children, I wanted to send them to good schools, and I thought *"If I'm going to retire on $50,000 per annum, I'm going to need a bigger bonus and savings,"* and I thought, *"I can't see myself ever getting any of those savings if I stay where I am."* That coincided with me reading *Rich Dad Poor Dad* by Robert Kiyosaki, that changed the paradigm considerably. I don't regret having done my Equine surgery training. I loved doing surgery and I still do, but I realised there's this big limitation in what I could ever produce with my own hands and I only had so many hands at the end of the day. I needed to become involved in a scenario where I was in a team and the whole team was producing rather than just me.

DIEDERIK: You moved back to Australia?

MARK: I looked for an opportunity to become a partner in a practice and I moved to Canberra Veterinary Hospital 15 years ago.

DIEDERIK: What didn't they teach you at vet school that they should have taught you in order to be more successful?

MARK: One of the really big things is not just the science in veterinary science, but a huge part is communication and being able to communicate not only with your teammates but particularly with the clients. Our whole reason for being is to be (and the community expects us to be) the greatest advocate for animals. That's our duty. But, unless we can communicate what we need to do for those animals to the client and bring them along on that journey, we're going to fail in our advocacy.

DIEDERIK: If you had a new graduate here and you wanted to help them turbocharge their career, what are some things would you tell them?

MARK: It's important that you learn to communicate, build rapport with the client, but also be clear and concise about what the animal needs. As veterinarians, sometimes, we're a little vague and we're hesitant to say *this* is what the animal needs, rather than give various options and recommendations which don't sound compelling, and then the client thinks maybe they're not that necessary. Meanwhile the animal misses out on what it needs, it deserves.

You've got to do the consulting well but, make sure that you learn to do surgery. Do not think that's something that has to be referred all the time. There's so much surgery that can be done in practice; there are many courses you can do. The same goes for things like ultrasonography. Practices these days need surgeons, ultrasonographers, and these are very valuable things to bring to a practice, and to your own sense of satisfaction in your career.

DIEDERIK: Same new graduate, what are one, two or three things that they should avoid?

MARK: Focus on those few things that are going to give you the best results in terms of career satisfaction. Ultimately, we're a poorly remunerated profession, that needs to change but, the antidote to that is within ourselves. We have to do more; we have to become more valuable as people in this clinical situation. So, focus on those things, communication and perhaps surgery and ultrasound, in case they're interested.

DIEDERIK: If you were doing this journey again, would you be a vet?

MARK: I would be a vet. I love my career. The thing about being a vet, is it's all about problem-solving, and it does put you in front of people, and people skills are important. And we are still masters of our destiny. Yes, there's pet insurance and what have you, but if you were, say, a medico then you've got the government to answer to, you've got health insurance companies to answer to.

DIEDERIK: From the outside, Dr Mark Ethell would seem to be a very successful person, awesome practice with a huge team. Undoubtedly, it hasn't come easily. What challenges have you faced?

MARK: The biggest thing is to get clear in your head what your vision is and what your goals are, and then don't become over-focused on them.

You might have used the word success somewhere in there, but success is whatever your definition of success is. I set about with certain goals to become a partner in a practice, etc. I wanted it to be successful in my terms, but I would say to any other human being, *"Well, just think really deeply about what it is that motivates you and what you want for your life. And, think about it, think about it often, and you will then work towards it."*

No matter what you do, there's going to be challenges and obstacles that slow you down, and you just have to remain focused. It's really, important to be persistent. A lot of people drop off along the journey because it's too hard, but you just have to always go that extra mile, and it's amazing what can happen.

DIEDERIK: A lot of practitioners that either work for someone else, or run a small practice, find it hard to balance work/life/family. Here you are in a huge practice with a really good balance—how do you do that?

MARK: There are big rocks in your life; there's your loved ones, other family members and friends, and keeping yourself healthy. You just have to keep all of those in balance. Again, it's process of – and I'm not perfect in this by any mean – so I'll go through stages and phases where one of those rocks gets more attention, it needs it for a period, and another one is not getting as much as it should. But as long as you're constantly thinking about it, you can keep it within balance. A big part of it, though, is to realise that actually this is a team sport, veterinary practice, and your life is a team sport. So, you need to have help, you need to realise that you can't be the chief cook and bottle washer for everything that happens in a business or elsewhere in your life as well. Delegation, asking for help, de-modification discussions are the way to do it.

DIEDERIK: If one of your children was here and said, *"Hey dad, I want a veterinary career"* what are a few things that you would tell?

MARK: I think the discussions are exactly the same as what I said when a new grad is sitting across from me. Thankfully, veterinary science gives you a whole wealth of opportunities, and so obviously, you need to be passionate about it.

DIEDERIK: What's your definition of success?

MARK: First and foremost, it's about my wife and family and then the extended family. That's central to everything, and life is the central bit. And then as they all age, it's time and money and having freedom for those things. For me, success is having time freedom and financial freedom.

DIEDERIK: What have been the keys to getting that to happen?

MARK: The key has been to organise the work side of things in such a way that it is balanced. Certainly, ownership in a veterinary practice is an obvious step towards that. However, there are plenty of others in veterinary practices that are slaves to those practices. So, once you own a veterinary practice, it is a matter of designing it to suit those needs.

DIEDERIK: Quit yourself out of those many roles as you can.

MARK: That was the plan and that was difficult; it was to make myself as redundant as possible. The first difficult step, was to wean myself away from 100% client contact, because the clients keep asking for you and you like doing it. At the end of the day, if you're going to grow your practice, you can't easily do that if you're always seeing clients. There's got to be some stepping back and work on the business and not just work in the business.

? DIEDERIK: That's an important point, the *E-Myth Revisited* – if you haven't read the *E-Myth* by Michael Gerber, do so.

You're always, 'up', motivated – how do you do that?

MARK: I don't know. I think it's just inherent. It's just built in.

? DIEDERIK: If you had the chance to do this again would you do anything differently?

MARK: I don't think so. I think my journey thus far has been really good. I've enjoyed it.

? DIEDERIK: What do you see holding most people back from achieving their goals?

MARK: A really important, one, is setting a goal. And then practice management is really important, but leadership is more important. Again, it's the leadership required to actually implement some of these things that is the missing link, in a lot of practices.

I see a number of practices, in which leadership is missing and they end up frustrated about poor profitability, teams causing grief, with HR issues and things like that, and we're just not dealing with them effectively. I think as an industry, we do that poorly.

? DIEDERIK: Has tragedy or luck played a part in what you've achieved?

MARK: Of course, luck is a very important part of it, having said that you do make your own luck. You put yourself in the right place at the right time, and who knows what that balance is. In life, there are actually lots of opportunities in front of us, we just have to be open to them to see them. I have suffered the problem where I've seen too many opportunities, and I had to remind myself to remain focused on those one, two or three that are important.

DIEDERIK: What pitfalls should a veterinarian who's wanting improvement avoid?

MARK: I don't know what they should avoid. I do know what they should be doing. It's an element of just having to step back to some extent and have a look at the bigger picture, and think strategically about your practice not just the day to day operations. We have been very lucky in the veterinary industry, that we've had very little competition. That's changing. I don't think we will get away with being as complacent as we have been in previous decades.

DIEDERIK: We've been very protected for a long time, and now those protections are being lost and most practices are not coping with that very well. What are you passionate about in veterinary science?

MARK: The business of veterinary science, because it involves engaging a team, developing your team to all be better as individuals, but then collectively to be really awesome. I think that that will produce satisfying careers for our people, it'll produce much better remunerating careers for our people, and I think those things are very average at the moment. That needs to change. I think the better we can do the business of veterinary science, the better off the animals will be, because if we look after them, then we can financially be better off and our teams will be better off also. They'll be more engaged, they'll have more satisfying careers and they'll be better paid and better off.

DIEDERIK: You've got a distinct compartmentalisation of the business and the clinical side of practice, when did you make that distinction?

MARK: It was the moment I read *Rich Dad Poor Dad* followed by the *E-Myth*, that it became clear that veterinary practice is a business.

? DIEDERIK: Our industry has a 'reputation', what is keeping you sane?

··· MARK: Having regular time off, going on holidays. You really do need to have a good break to stay fresh. And, having loved ones that you can share those times with.

? DIEDERIK: What's the biggest thing you have given back to the community?

··· MARK: That happens on a lot of levels.

Thankfully, in veterinary practice, providing the very best medicine also results in the best business results. We are able to provide the best animal welfare, the best animal results as far as health and well-being goes, and that correlates with success financially. That correlates with our teams being better off and being happier. In addition, there is some level of surplus money, to some extent, which means that we can then take in those cases that help the community such as wildlife, stray animals and that sort of thing all because the rest of the organisation runs well.

? DIEDERIK: Have you got three secrets or takeaways?

··· MARK: We've probably covered them. It's really important to develop as an individual. In our practice, we have a core purpose, the reason why we do what we do, and we have a vision for where we want to head, and we have core values. I am a really big believer in doing that as an individual too.

As an individual, we should think deeply about what our core purpose in life is, and what our core values are and think deeply about those things and then drive towards the goals which are consistent with that. That's the key. Most of us don't take the time to do that.

DIEDERIK: What do you see is the future of the Australian veterinary industry?

MARK: I'm excited about the potential...It won't be without some headwinds. If we stick to our core purpose, and stick to our core values and implement those well, we will set ourselves apart from much of the competition, and our organisations will flourish.

At the end of the day, pet ownership might be declining, in percentage terms. But those pets are undoubtedly becoming more and more important to their families and expectation for their care and medical care is increasing all the time so I think there will be a market.

I guess the same with the animal industries too. There'll always be a market for that. Obviously, from the global stance, food is going to become increasingly more important, and Australia is very fortunate to have the resources we do. There's a lot of upside for us there.

We've got unique skills; we need to value ourselves better and we need to sell ourselves better.

DIEDERIK: Was there ever a defining moment, a snap point, a line in the sand?

MARK: I can't think of any in particular. I can think of lots of little ones...probably not a big one.

The biggest paradigm shift, was when I was in academia, I passed my American Boards to become a specialist, that was a big milestone in my career that was very hard to achieve. Then I read those two important books; that turned my whole world upside down. That was a defining moment.

DIEDERIK: Mark, thank you very much.

Key Take-Aways

- It's really, important that you learn to communicate, build rapport with the client, but also be clear and concise about what the animal needs

- Focus on those few things that are going to give you the best bang for your buck in terms of career satisfaction

- Just think deeply about what it is that motivates you and what you want for your life. And, think about it, think about it often, and you will then work towards it

- Veterinary science gives you a whole wealth of opportunities, and so obviously, you need to be passionate about it

- I'm passionate about the business of veterinary science, and I'm passionate about that because it involves engaging a team, developing your teams to be all better as individuals, but then collectively to be awesome

> **"Veterinarians – a highly protected industry and we're rapidly losing those protections and now we have to compete in a commercial market place on a more level playing field."**
>
> Diederik Gelderman

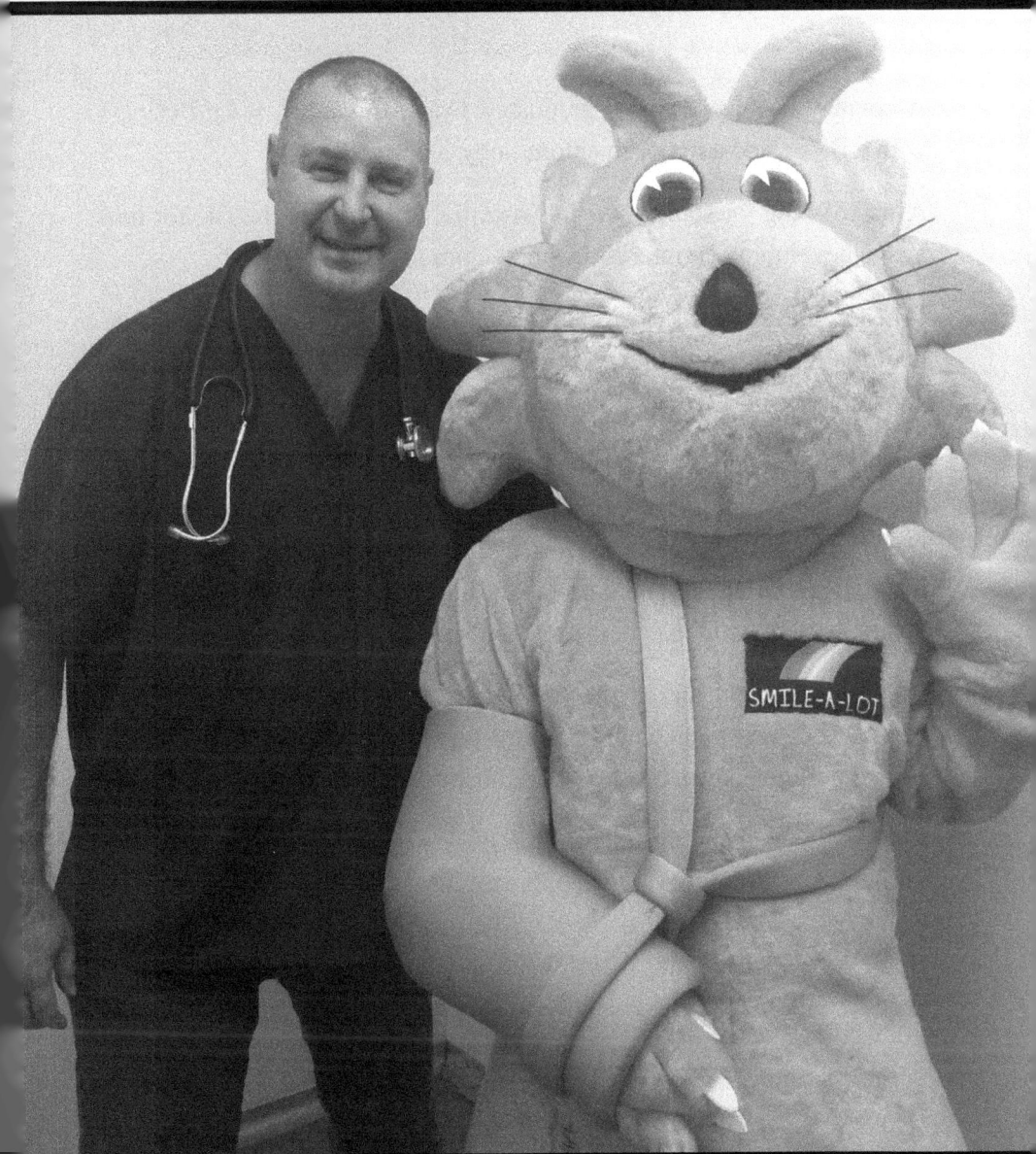

Dr Rob Hill

Dr Rob Hill

BVSc

> *"Ever consider what pets must think of us? I mean, here we come back from a grocery store with the most amazing haul – chicken, pork, half a cow. They must think we're the greatest hunters on earth!"* ~ Anne Tyler

A country boy from NSW, graduated from University of Qld (1995) with a BVSc and a major in entomology.

After working for some years in Australia, Rob went to the UK for five years, developing an interest in small animals.

When homesickness kicked in, he backpacked back to Australia where he initially leased and then purchased a practice in Australind, Western Australia.

During this period, Rob married Lisa and they lived in the shed at the back of the hospital. They had three children and finally moved away from the hospital. After years of struggle, he sought consultancy advice from Diederik Gelderman who taught him the principles of successful business. Slowly the business grew.

Rob and his team turned the old house into 'The Happiness Centre' which went on to become an award-winning business. In 2016 Rob started building a new purpose-built hospital at Treendale.

Rob is also a published author (*The Winner's Code*) and the Smile-A-Lot personal development series for young children. Rob has now also started a business consultancy service. He believes that nothing worthwhile in life is ever easy and that one needs resilience and perseverance to succeed.

DIEDERIK: What ignited your passion to become a vet and at what age did you make that decision Rob?

ROB: Like most teenagers, I didn't know what I wanted to do. I didn't really have a calling.

I was conflicted between following a path into physiotherapy that my sporting interests had stirred or following my love for animals into the veterinary profession. As with many things in life, when you lack clarity, I played the hand I was dealt.

You need absolute clarity around what you actually want in life, to avoid being drawn in different directions and floating like a feather at the mercy of the winds.

DIEDERIK: What didn't they teach you in vet school that you know now is crucial to your success as a practising veterinarian.

ROB: Graduates of the era weren't taught well at all. New graduates were like lambs to the slaughter. They were poorly finished, had limited surgical and clinical experience and were poorly supported. The modern graduate is better educated and better connected to information via the internet and modern technologies.

Vets should have lectures on business, or at least have subjects that explain their place in making a business profitable.

Too many vets have a poverty mindset. Talking about money and performance makes them toxic towards the owner and the business and manifests as poor performance and becomes a malignancy to the team culture.

Vets need to learn about business. The profession attracts high achievers who limit their own success through a poor mindset and a negative attitude to money.

If you want to succeed in veterinary business, you need a business education. This may involve using mentors and coaches.

Personal development beyond veterinary education is essential.

The game-changer for me in business was leadership training.

DIEDERIK: What did they teach you in vet school which proved to be incorrect in the real world?

ROB: Veterinary schools are teaching to the highest standards available during the era in which the student was trained. Their objective is to turn out veterinarians and they do a good job of that. They could arguably turn out people with a more rounded education in life skills.

DIEDERIK: What are three things that a new graduate must do immediately to 'turbocharge' his/her veterinary career?

ROB: The first essential requirement is to have the courage to try more difficult procedures and to keep learning and adding to your skillset.

The second must be to develop a specialty.

If you want to become truly great at any business in your life, you must learn how to sell. Sales training is crucial. Learn to sell, get over the fear of rejection and develop good attitudes to money.

DIEDERIK: What are the three things that a new graduate must avoid to turbocharge his/her career?

ROB: Avoid negative people. They have a problem for every solution.

Avoid cheap practices. They will attract clients that will never let you diagnose and fix anything and they certainly won't be spending money on your personal development.

Avoid the profession in your personal time. Make connections with different professional and business people in the community.

DIEDERIK: If you were starting again would you in fact be a vet?

ROB: No. I wouldn't be a vet again. I am proud of what I have achieved from my very humble beginnings in life. I have travelled the world and learnt about business and been exposed to some remarkable people. I have worked too much and too hard though and I have not acquired the riches to allow me to make up for lost time. My veterinary career has come at the expense of time with my children. I will never get that time back either and I will live with regret.

DIEDERIK: What were three major challenges that you faced?

ROB: The biggest hurdle was the venom from the public about veterinary fees. I had to develop coping strategies to deal with the public and the constant negotiation and justification of our fees.

Our business start-up was challenging. I was working 12 hours a day as a sole practitioner seven days a week and then having to do the business work and be on call. That was five years of absolute hell to be honest.

Hiring the right people, training and motivating them was a real challenge and a learning curve.

DIEDERIK: How did you manage to balance family, career and fatherhood?

ROB: I have not attained work–life balance, to the detriment of my family and to my health. At the time of this interview, we are about to open our incredibly beautiful hospital. I'm hoping that life balance and quality family time will finally become a reality.

DIEDERIK: What five things would you advise your son or daughter if they were about to embark on a veterinary career?

ROB: None of my children will be veterinarians. I will make sure they don't become vets

DIEDERIK: What is your definition of success?

ROB: I consider myself a high achiever so that is a difficult question to answer because the goal posts are constantly moving. When I matriculated, I felt successful. When I passed my exams each semester, I felt successful. When I graduated, I felt successful. When I started my business, I felt successful. I have survived 15 years in business which makes me feel successful. We have won multiple business awards and I feel successful. I married my lovely wife and had three beautiful children which makes me feel successful. I have built the practice of my dreams which makes me feel successful.

Success is about being able to support my family as the bottom line, but I also expect more of myself.

What is success to me now? The Rob of his late-forties sees success as achieving your goals whilst attaining a balance in life.

DIEDERIK: What do you think is or are your biggest successes?

ROB: My greatest success is having a lovely family and being able to support them, educate my children at a nice school, being able to pay the bills and provide them with gifts on important occasions. This is what matters to me. This is paradoxically why I have driven myself so hard to be able to provide for my wife and children.

We have just completed one of the largest and most beautiful veterinary hospitals in Australia. This completion is one of our biggest successes. To make this hospital successful is our next challenge.

DIEDERIK: What are or were the keys to these successes?

ROB: The number one key is persistence. If you just keep going, you get somewhere.

Personal growth has been very important. I had to change, and to grow.

The third key was CANI! Constant and Never Ending Improvement. I have made every mistake there is to make. Most people see failures as failures. I see failures as learnings.

Anything I have achieved, I have achieved through the support of my wife. She has been with me for the entire journey, and at times has been the only friend I had. She has helped me through some very difficult and dark times when the world seemed against me.

DIEDERIK: What are the best methods or strategies for keeping oneself motivated and focused?

ROB: There have certainly been times where I have struggled for motivation. The long days and weeks without any break from the grind and even years at a time without holidays has driven me to the abyss of personal sanity at times. I have lost focus at times and it's always disastrous.

The best way to keep motivated is to set goals. Big, hairy, audacious goals as well as short term achievable goals. You need to build a 'staircase' to the big goal with smaller achievable goals that will take you towards what you want. Everything is achievable if you break it down into small enough tasks. The challenge is to have patience and the commitment to stay on track.

DIEDERIK: If you had the chance to do it all again, what would you do differently?

ROB: I would set up a veterinary hospital in a more affluent area. I definitely would not buy the second business that tipped me over the edge into a deep depression.

If I could start all over again, I wouldn't be a vet, or I would have given it away after my first few months in practice.

Some industries make money and some don't. The veterinary industry is not a wonderful business model. Yes, you can make a decent living and some people who scale their business do quite well. It is possible to become wealthy as a vet but most don't.

DIEDERIK: What do you think holds most vets back from achieving their goals?

ROB: Many vets have a poverty mindset. For business owners, the poverty mindset of the employee vets can hold their businesses back.

Ego can get in the way of a vet as well. Many vets have egos so big it gets in their way. They know everything. They won't be told anything.

The other major problem for owners is that they are so busy working 'in' the business, that they spend virtually no time working 'on' the business. They are so busy doing everything 'properly' that they don't leverage themselves. They get in their own way because nobody can do it as well as they can.

Poor management is an endemic feature across the industry. Most veterinary managers were veterinary nurses, and they may have been great nurses but they are terrible managers.

Owner-managers are also a disaster. I've done it both through necessity and by choice. You can't. Hire a GREAT manager if you want your business to be successful. If you can't afford one, let go staff until you can and start again with a great manager. They pay for themselves.

? DIEDERIK: Do you think that tragedy or luck has played a part in you achieving your success?

… ROB: It's funny how the harder you work, the luckier you get. I took a calculated risk on the location I chose and the practice I bought. My luck was that a friend of mine from University told me about it, so I guess there was an element of luck. I saw the potential though and the next 15 years were a really hard slog. Hard work and persistence makes you 'lucky'.

There has certainly been some tragedy as well. I bounced back from a mental breakdown and a failed business expansion.

I went through an extraordinary time of personal growth which gave me the strength and confidence to do things better. I also started to challenge the paradigms of the industry. We started a 'Happiness Centre' and engaged our community in a remarkable concept of extraordinary innovations that nobody had ever done in veterinary science before. Despite the scepticisms and cynicism of some staff and some clients, it was an extraordinary success.

? DIEDERIK: If you were helping someone else, what pitfalls should they make sure that they avoid?

… ROB: Hire slow and fire fast. Your success is determined by the team you hire. Your staff need to contribute to your vision and be supportive of you. Treat them well and train them, but equally, get rid of the ones that overtly disrespect you in your own business.

NOTE: You can find the remainder of this interview online at:

www.VeterinarySuccessSecretsRevealed.com

Key Take-Aways

- You need absolute clarity around what you want in life, to avoid being drawn in different directions and floating like a feather at the mercy of the winds

- Vets should have lectures on business, or at least have subjects that explain their place in making a business profitable

- The wall flowers who won't learn anything difficult and want to refer everything so they don't make a mistake are on the unwavering path of mediocrity

- Truly successful people rarely have a bad word to say about other people and will usually be gracious enough to help you succeed

- When your brain focuses on positive things, you are mentally brighter and more creative and the answers to the questions you seek will appear from your subconscious

Note: Rob and I did not perform a live interview – he responded to my questions via email.

> **"You need to make a profit from the 'core' of your Veterinary business and not rely on the 'cream' like merchandising, over the counter sales and sales of medicines. Not to do this is plain folly."**
>
> Diederik Gelderman

Dr Sam Bowden

Dr Sam Bowden

BVSc

> *"If having a soul means being able to feel love and loyalty and gratitude, then animals are better off than a lot of humans".* ~ James Herriot

Sam Bowden graduated from the University of Queensland in 1996 and spent 15 years as a practicing veterinarian. In this time, he owned two practices, each of which achieved phenomenal results, both in terms of practice growth and profitability.

Sam saw an industry that was fighting itself through a lack of unification, which resulted in low profit and high stress for the vets in that industry. He therefore started the United Veterinary Group in 2010. He used this as a platform to educate and allow fellow vets to interact and share business ideas.

Sam Bowden has devoted his last 11 years to helping practice owners increase their happiness, work–life balance and profitability after he went from near bankruptcy to creating financial freedom and an extraordinary lifestyle in a few short years.

DIEDERIK: What ignited your passion to become a vet Sam, and at what age did that start?

SAM: I wasn't your traditional vet who loved to be a vet. I grew up on a sheep and cattle station; I was at University and someone said, *"What do you want to do?",* I got the list of degrees and pretty much threw a dart at it and landed on vet.

DIEDERIK: What didn't they teach you at Uni, that you now know is crucial to your success as a veterinarian?

SAM: What they taught us was all very theoretical and technical. I was one of those people who wanted to be an entrepreneur, I was always going to be a practice owner and they didn't teach me was the realities of what it takes to be a practice owner or the mindset for success.

What they didn't teach us was success science; what it is that you need, how is it you need to think, and what it is you need to do to be successful – irrespective of what you work as.

DIEDERIK: If you had a new graduate sitting here, what are three things that you're going to tell them to do to turbocharge their career?

SAM: The first thing is I would get them to write what I call their 'story'. Which is a letter to themselves as if they're writing it in a years' time. For example; *"It's November 2017. What an amazing year I have experienced. This is what's happened."* We're writing down the future of what I would like to happen. We cover professional development, skillsets, health, relationships, finances and spirituality. The first thing that I get them to do is understand that the human brain creates the future, it manifests the future.

Secondly, I would get them to start personal development by starting to read; *Big Leap,* or *Think and Grow Rich* – something on the mindset of success science.

Thirdly, I would give them dedicated work time to develop those skills and I would be happy to mentor them early on as long as they're moving forward. Obviously, I'd have someone teach them veterinary skills as well – that's first and foremost. But, self-esteem and how you see yourself is so important in whether you become a great vet.

❓ DIEDERIK: This new graduate that you're mentoring, are there a couple of things that you're going to tell them they need to avoid doing?

💬 SAM: Number one is comparing themselves to anybody else.

Low esteem, one of the greatest ways to do that is compare yourself to someone else. The goal is just to say each day, *"Did I do my best?"* One of the things that pressures new grads is this massive fear of getting something wrong.

And we talk about progression, not perfection. *"Did you get a little bit better this week? Or today than yesterday?"*

Then I would teach them consult room skills, as in how you actually consult to get money out of the equation, give them a format to follow that allows them to overcome the fear of talking to people about money.

❓ DIEDERIK: If you were starting again, would you actually be a vet?

💬 SAM: I love the concept of precession. It says that, *"It doesn't matter what you're doing. As long as you're in forward momentum, you'll end up where you're meant to end up."*

If I look at the skillsets that I've got, does that make me cross adaptable to a myriad of different industries? I have seen so many vets who have chosen to exit the profession and have gone to be very successful outside of the profession because the skillsets we learn really set you up to be a be great leader in any part of life.

❓ DIEDERIK: What were three major challenges you faced?

💬 SAM: Three major challenges.

In the early years, it's *"How the hell do I treat this animal?"*

I was lucky to have a supportive boss. If someone's coming out, I would say that that's important to make sure that first environment you're going to, make sure there is support.

Then came *"How do I manage my team?"*

And the third was when I exited my practice, the fear that I had around that. I only got through it because of my mentors.

DIEDERIK: How did you balance career, family, fatherhood?

SAM: It's called 'discipline', the discipline of working a four-day work week, and having *"The fifth day is for me or the family,"* and I didn't do weekends.

A lot of my success came from not working, not being on the tools where you start thinking and going to conferences, etc. That's where I got my ideas that actually made the difference.

The discipline around holidays, I book them in at the start of the year.

And here's the other thing, it's just having the discipline there that when you've got young family and you've got a business, naturally, as the provider, you sort of go *"Well, I need to spend more time in the business,"* and that's okay but, you've got a partner there, and I think the trap is that when we let our partner 'suffer' because of the business. I just think you just have to find a way to go, *"I'll do all three"*.

So, I think the number one lesson is actually discipline. You will always get pulled. There's pulling from your partner, or you don't have enough time at home. There's pull from your work, where there's more to do there at work. I think it's important to realise, Diederik, that you're never going to get through everything at work. That concept doesn't exist. So, it's important to say at the end of the day, *"Did I do the best that I could?"* Fantastic.

Celebrate. Go home. Enjoy your family. Come back. Start the next plan, and I think that's the discipline.

The other discipline is planning, so I can know what's going to happen, outcomes are more predictable.

DIEDERIK: What does success look like to you?

SAM: Success for me is feeling content and fulfilled. *"Do I feel successful across all contexts? Am I, do I feel balanced?"*

Am I healthy? Do I feel fit? Do I have time to go surfing, or going to gym or skiing, etc. Do I have time and presence with my family? Do I help get the kids ready in the morning, or put them to bed at night? Or during weekends, do I go and do fun things with them and be 'present'? Am I financially increasing each year?

Secondly, one of my greatest successes comes from my greatest failures; I bought another business and I didn't manage it very well, and I lost hundreds of thousands of dollars, and it pushed me to a place of depression and despair.

I had a mentor who said, *"This will make you very successful and this can give you two things. One, if you learn the lesson, and number two, if you get up and go again."*

So, when you feel like things aren't going so great just ask; *"What am I learning here?"*

Secondly, just seeing how my children are alive and well in life. I feel very successful there. They're very balanced.

I'd have to say on financial success, I've reached the place that I set out to get to 20 years ago, of complete financial freedom, which is I don't need to work, my passive income provides me with as much money as we would need.

? DIEDERIK: You're a motivated and focused person; how do you maintain that?

SAM: You've actually got to love what you do. I think having a passion so that every day I look to go, *"How can I do something that's selfless to actually help someone else?"*

Learning the concept of leverage and learning to let go of things as you move to the next level, which is always the challenge because 'I'm the only person who can do it' and teach someone else and move to the next level.

Number three, creating the life that I want. When you don't like things that are happening, if you take the view that life's happening for you, not to you, then everything's a gift.

I always look at the things that I can be grateful for but I had to learn that as a skillset because it wasn't natural for me. I used to be the doom and gloom boy, I used to worry a lot, and I've had to teach myself to catch my own thoughts and think, *"Well that's not actually true,"* and think of the brightness of the future.

? DIEDERIK: Give us two ideas of what holds most vets back from achieving their goals?

NOTE: You can find Sam's answer to this question and the remainder of this interview online at:

www.VeterinarySuccessSecretsRevealed.com

Key Take-Aways

- What they didn't teach us at Uni was success science

- Self-esteem and how you see yourself is so important in ensuring that you become a great vet

- Never compare yourself to anyone else, just compare yourself to yourself. And the goal is just to say each day, *"Did I do my best?"*

- Get mentors as early on as you can to help you with your mindset and belief systems. This will save you many years and many hundreds of thousands of dollars in time, effort and pain

- The number one lesson is actually discipline. You will always get pulled; your partner, or you don't have enough time at home, from your work. It's important to realise that you're never going to get everything done

> **"It would be much better for our industry if we vets suffered more pain from going broke and failing in our business – at least that way, more of us would be forced to take action and do something about it."**
>
> Diederik Gelderman

Dr Shannon Coyne

Shannon Coyne

BVSc (Hons)

> *"Old age means realising you will never own all the dogs you wanted to."* ~ Joe Gores

Shannon was born in Central Queensland, attended the University of Queensland and graduated in 1998.

After graduation, he worked in mixed practice for two years. Then came twelve months locuming in the UK, also largely in mixed practice. He was driven out by the cold.

By mistake, he moved to Gympie in 2002 as the fifth vet in a mixed practice. In 2004 he bought into the practice, which is now a ten-vet practice.

He says that his number one achievement is; a wonderful family.

He believes that the practice's standard of care is increasing year to year and he is proud of his part in this development, even though the entire team from partners to cleaners have made it happen.

He is still in practice and loving it and has four success tips:

1. Find a place that lets you practice to the standard you are proud of.

2. Great workmates help in every aspect.

3. Employ a manager who excels where you can't.

4. When you find a place that lets you develop and provides the lifestyle you need; it is worth digging in roots and working hard.

DIEDERIK: Shannon, what ignited your passion to become a vet, and at what age did that occur?

SHANNON: Early high school. I got a pretty typical...'left high school, love the idea of being a vet, went to Uni, graduated', so no mature age kind of study or anything like that.

I loved science at school, loved animals, I loved problem-solving in my school work, and it just seemed a great career where you got to use your brain, use your hands and it all sort of gelled together. That was sort of what excited me and what sort of kept me going.

DIEDERIK: What didn't they teach you at vet school, and you're now in a mixed animal, regional practice, that you should have been taught at Uni?

SHANNON: Clients don't necessarily want a definitive diagnosis. As vets, we love it. That's what gets us out of bed in the morning; getting to the bottom and getting the answer. The clients just want a plan, a problem solved, and if you can put fancy name on it that's fantastic, but they just want to know *"I'm going to take this medication, you expect things to improve in two days, and if they don't come back and we'll change tack and we'll get it better."*

DIEDERIK: The other side of that coin, what did they teach you at Uni which you now know to be incorrect in the real world of veterinary medicine?

SHANNON: The main thing I would say was incorrect – that clients, particularly our clients, but all clients are very money driven and you've rarely ever got enough money behind you to run every test that's recommended. Apart from, perhaps, some insured dog. You have just got the 'basics'. Even bloods and x-rays are too expensive for many. So, you have to really use your brain to nut things out. So...don't rely on those tests.

? DIEDERIK: If you had a new grad sitting here, what are two or three things that you'd suggest he or she do immediately to turbocharge their career?

SHANNON: Number one: find a practice that's going to allow you to do the things that you think that you'd like to do, in the area that you'd like to work in. Go there for a couple of years, and then move, get a different perspective. Don't get bogged down in one practice.

The second thing; every chance you get, do the things that you don't particularly like. I hated dentistry, and I was rubbish at it. So, I went and did – every conference that I went to, I started on the dental lectures. I was rubbish with it, and I did a post-grad foundation course. I still don't like them but they're just part of the job now, and I'm not scared of them.

? DIEDERIK: The flip side of that coin, what are two or three things they've got to avoid or avoid doing to turbocharge their career?

SHANNON: Don't get locked into that *"Oh, I'm just going to vaccinate dogs"*. You've got to be taking your cases and running with them. Don't get locked into that *"It's a fractured bone so I've got to hand it over"*. If it's a fractured bone, you've got to be scrubbing in with the surgeon. Grab your cases and run with them.

? DIEDERIK: If you were starting over again, would you in fact be a vet?

SHANNON: I would. I've never come across anything else that would take its place. I probably would try something different. If I had the option, I'd probably say, *"Well, I've gone this far, maybe I'd be an academic or research or something completely different,"* but I think the veterinary industry is where I'd still be.

DIEDERIK: What were three significant challenges that you've faced in your career?

SHANNON: The first thing that made me want to chuck the life would be that point that most new grads get to where you're one or two years out, you're physically and mentally exhausted and you're sole charge, and you've got grumpy clients. We all get to it, and we just want to chuck it in, and that weighed pretty heavily on me, easily, the first ten years of my career. It was just that *"Uh...I'm coming back on-call, I'm sole charge, I've got...in 150k radius, I'm the only vet in the whole place..."* and that's a big stress.

Other than that, it's learning on your feet.

DIEDERIK: How did you balance your family, your career and fatherhood?

SHANNON: I have a very understanding wife and family, so that helped a lot. They know that, there's going to be problems when you're not going to be seeing me for a week. It's just a bad part of life. Every practice I've worked for, I guess, knows that that's terrible, certainly we do. We aim for big breaks, clear your head and big breaks with the family. The only part of it is just understanding that that's the career and that there's going to be ups and downs.

DIEDERIK: What does success look like to you?

SHANNON: Personal success, would be, life-wise, having a happy family and having time to enjoy my family and being able to go and do leisure activities. The work component, success is having and being confident and happy with the service I can provide, having that really happy work place. We've got to be a good team and we've got to be able to provide a great service and be proud of what we provide.

❓ DIEDERIK: What have been the keys to those successes?

💬 SHANNON: The keys have been my colleagues. I'm the one being interviewed, but the partners that we've have in Gympie here for our career, we've all worked together, we know we have our ups and own like every partnership, but they've been the key. We've all had a similar goal, and we've all worked hard and expanded, and no one has dragged the chain. When I joined the practice, the practice fundamentally was very good. The rules in place when I joined are still the rules in place now as far as the partners go, and it's worked really well.

Definitely family. I have got that good family support in all sort of matters, for sure.

And the location. I came into the practice in a growth phase, and the town's in a growth phase. It was seeing early that *"Look, this place is going to grow. We've just got to hang on and go for the ride because there is going to be a career here,"* and spotting that and sitting tight.

❓ DIEDERIK: Keeping yourself motivated, what are the best methods that you found?

💬 SHANNON: When we get that fatigue, everyone in the practice goes through it, we just have a big long holiday block, and just getting that fresh air when you get that fatigue. If you're starting to get a little bit bored, or in a rut, then CPD, whether it's just a conference, whether it's going and doing an external course, or even sometimes going to visit another practice for a week. I really enjoy that, and you come back and think *"We can do this, this, and this better."* Just clear the head and get a different perspective and go again.

DIEDERIK: If you had the chance to do it again, what would you do differently if anything?

SHANNON: My career, if I wasn't lucky enough to find this place, I probably would have travelled a bit more and perhaps done a little bit more – perhaps gotten memberships, if we're close to the city, maybe fellowship, because I really enjoy my surgery.

Certainly, we would have gotten our practice manager in earlier. Someone who can do the stuff that we're not very good at, that would have been a better choice, and that would have taken a lot of the early stress off and grown the practice a lot quicker.

DIEDERIK: You obviously think that luck has played a big part in how you sort of fell into Gympie as it were. Any other luck or tragedy that has played a part?

SHANNON: Not really. Certainly, it's good to have a brother who's a vet, who can say, *"Look, that's a good. That's good, that's not good."* Having advice from someone a bit older is a great help. Other than that, it really is just sort of stumbling into a town, which was a complete mistake. My wife and I just came back from the UK working over there. I was definitely going for a job two hours north of Brisbane, and I said to her, *"That's Noosa, we'll take that. I'd love to work at Noosa."* We were looking for a place to settle, and then we got this reply from employment agency, *"Gympie wants to interview you."* And I said, *"I never applied for Gympie."* And she said, *"Actually, you did."* And we came in, and I said to my wife, *"Look, six to twelve months. We'll just sit tight for six to twelve months, get our feet and then we'll go somewhere else."* Yeah, it suited us down to the ground so we're still here. It was great.

? DIEDERIK: What holds most vets back from achieving their goals?

SHANNON: Part of it is…it is a stressful job and a fatiguing job, and a lot of the day-to-day business grinds people down. People tend to get trapped in that rut and not look at the long-term career just because they're bogged down and they're not prepared, or they're too tired then to make time.

Also, it's certainly an industry where the financial rewards aren't particularly there. And a lot of people then get depressed and a little bit down on the industry, and then get out before really settling in. If you can get through that, and remind yourself you're doing what you like and take advantage of some of that CPD and find a niche. You've just got to get through that rough time and find the spot that you like.

? DIEDERIK: What pitfalls would you point out, should they avoid when they go into practice?

NOTE: You can find Shannon's answer to this question and the remainder of this interview online at:

www.VeterinarySuccessSecretsRevealed.com

Key Take-Aways

- Choose a practice where you'll get to do the things that you really like doing
- Force yourself to do the things that you don't like and are not good at, this is the way to learn
- Success is having and being confident and happy with the service I can provide, having that really happy work place and a balanced family life

- When you get fatigued, take a (big, long) break, clear your head and go again
- There's a fine line between working hard and learning, and working too hard and burning yourself.

> **"Veterinarian! You need to learn to value yourself and your expertise".**
>
> Diederik Gelderman

Dr Vera Pickering

Dr Vera Pickering

BVSc, (Hons)

> *"At his best, man is the noblest of all animals; separated from law and justice he is the worst."* ~ Aristotle

Vera grew up in Adelaide and moved to attend Sydney University, graduating in 1974.

After working in a few veterinary practices, she bought into Mona Vale Veterinary Hospital in 1977. Vera then bought another veterinary practice in Avalon in 1982. In 1988, Vera was a founding member of Northside Emergency Veterinary Service.

Vera built up Mona Vale Vets into the busy practice it is today and is recognised as being one of the pillars of the veterinary community on the Northern Beaches. She handed over the ownership reigns in 2012 but continues to be actively involved in the life of MVVH.

Her current veterinary interests include animal behaviour. Vera is also very involved in mentoring students and supports.

Having lessened her veterinary workload, Vera has loaded her timetable up with fun and creative things; sailing on Pittwater, walking, cooking, reading, the theatre and she has recently taken up watercolour painting. These activities are enhanced by listening to music.

Vera has two daughters, Tania and Claudia. Her current pet family includes Bobby the Boxer; Jai the Golden Retriever; two cats, Louis and Archie; and eight chickens.

DIEDERIK: So Vera, let me ask, what ignited your passion to become a vet, and what age did you make that decision?

VERA: It wasn't a passion. I didn't think of it until three-quarters of the way through first year Uni Adelaide where I was doing marine biology, and thinking *"Well, I couldn't get the job that I wanted"* – which was up on an underwater research station – *"unless I was one of the top 2 in Australia, so what else can I do?"* Well, I could do engineering because I like maths and things like that, but I won't do that because my uncle and my grandfather are engineers. I don't want to compete. I could do medicine because I like biology, well, no I won't do that because my grandmother always wanted me to be a doctor. I was contrary, and I thought *"Gee, Vet Science would be good."* I used to spend all my weekends on a farm that belongs to friends of my family, and so I thought, *"Vet Science would be fun, wouldn't it? And it will get me out of Adelaide. I could go to Sydney, Melbourne or Brisbane."* So, I applied for a scholarship and bugger me, I got it, then I told my family.

DIEDERIK: Looking back, what didn't they teach at Uni that you know now is crucial to being a successful practicing veterinarian?

VERA: I think they don't teach you enough to listen and observe, to listen to the humans that are bringing their animals or describing the condition. And the importance of listening to people and listening to the animals that you're dealing with. I'm using the word *'listening'* in a broader sense.

DIEDERIK: The other side of that coin is what did they teach you at Uni that once into the cold hard light of daily practice, was proven to be incorrect?

VERA: Well, at Uni, you sort of get taught that there's this one path to get the result that you have to get for a particular condition, and that sure as hell isn't true.

DIEDERIK: You've got a new graduate sitting down in front of you, what are two or three things you'd tell them to do immediately to turbocharge their career?

VERA: Be bold and try new procedures or treatment. Keep educated and read worldly, even outside of veterinary science necessarily. Be prepared to approach and put forward a new business idea or offer of a partnership even if it's not on the table.

DIEDERIK: And then the other side of that coin, what are three things they've got to avoid doing?

VERA: Staying in an environment where you're not happy with your work progression, or you're not happy with your work mates. Believing that the education you receive at Uni was the pinnacle and that there's nothing better. And staying in a rut with medications or procedures.

DIEDERIK: Your answers are really interesting. If you were starting again, and you were in first year biology, would you in fact be a vet in retrospect?

VERA: Likely yes or no. I don't know. I think I could have done many things and been perfectly happy.

DIEDERIK: What were three challenges you faced in the practice?

VERA: Being a female in a male-dominated profession (I finished in '74) and it was mostly blokes and practice owners were blokes. Another challenge was that my first vet partner decided to leave with three months' notice two days after the birth of my second child. And then some two or three years later, being given a month's notice of termination of lease of the premises.

DIEDERIK: They're fairly interesting challenges. You mentioned your second child, how did you manage to balance a really successful practice, with family career and motherhood in general?

VERA: I didn't find that particularly easy. You've just got to get organised. I employed a housekeeper a few days a week. It got a bit overbearing with the after hours stuff when I had...because I had three kids at home.

That's how the after-hours sprung to life in Sydney, because I approached Don Turner who lived up the road. I approached him because I had this great idea about how to setup an after-hours and make everybody want to join it in the local area. I put forward a proposal and we had a meeting with 25 vets and six weeks later, we started because I had answered all their questions, and not give them any problems or cost them any money, really, so how could you say no. Basically, if you put a proposal to somebody they can't say no to, they won't.

DIEDERIK: On a personal level, what is success? What does it look like?

VERA: Feeling that I've done some good at the end of every day.

DIEDERIK: What do you think is or are your biggest success in general terms?

VERA: Building up a practice to being a good-size practice. Designing and building and rebuilding the premises. Starting partnerships and getting far along in them. Raising successful, happy children. They've been my successes.

DIEDERIK: And, the keys to those successes, Vera?

VERA: Having a positive can-do outlook. Being willing to solve problems in new ways. Being persistent and nice to people, although firm. Knowing one's mind, but being prepared to change if something is not working. And, listening to others and trying their ideas if appropriate.

DIEDERIK: Thank you. Whenever I hear about you or read about you, or talk to you – you're always one of these people who is motivated and focused. What has kept you like that for such a long period of time?

VERA: I have no idea. I know I have a developed sense of responsibility, that probably helps. It's not something I've tried to develop, but it just is. I think as a teenager, I can remember my grandmother saying to me *"It uses less facial muscles, and therefore, you'll get less wrinkles if you smile, rather than frown."* So, I used to practice smiling in front of the mirror. You know what, if you do smile, you make yourself feel happier. And if you have a belief in you that, basically, life is good – which I do believe – and it will work out in the end, it's really helpful.

I don't know, it's just the way my brain is, and I have had my fair share of shit in life, I must say. But, yeah, I believe that basically, life is good. We're in a very lucky country, and we're in a very lucky situation, and *"Hey, there's always food on the table, a roof over my head, and I work at it, I can do stuff."*

DIEDERIK: If you had the chance to do this journey again, would you do anything differently?

VERA: I always think there's not enough time to work on all the myriads of projects that would be great to do, and I don't mean just veterinary science, you know, other things. But, the one thing we seem to run out of is time, in a sense, and I would spend more time with friends and develop more friendships with other humans.

DIEDERIK: You've achieved a lot of goals, what do you think holds most vets back from achieving their goals?

VERA: Not taking opportunities as they come up. Opportunities come to everybody, but most people don't take them. It's being complacent, not running with new or different ideas due to the fears of not succeeding, when one can always change again. It's the fear of failure or losing face and getting bogged down with minutiae instead of looking at a big picture.

I don't have a big ego, I think that helps, because I don't actually worry about what other people think of me. I just try to be honest and give things a go and have fun doing it. But, not taking opportunities is the biggest thing because there are opportunities everywhere and you've just got to grab them with both hands and run with it.

DIEDERIK: Has luck or tragedy has played any part in you achieving your success?

VERA: That's a really hard one. You know, opportunities come for everyone, and some of them you make for yourself.

I bought a house in a suburb and I walked into a practice in the suburb and said, *"How about I buy half of this practice because it's really convenient for me because I just live down the road, and I can give you some time off."* I mean, how ballsy is that? And I think about it now and I just laugh, but what was I going to lose? Nothing. How am I going to get 25 practices to be willing to work to get them cooperatively and be happy about it. You put forward a proposal and give it a go.

I must say, like a lot of happy people, I had an unhappy marriage, and personal things, I think, create much bigger problems in one's life. That did make me focus really, really hard on making the practice work, to continue to innovate and succeed so that I could support my family financially. But I was doing that and had been relatively successful, but for all that, that just made me focus even harder, I guess, and take less time off.

I think I've been pretty lucky, just, generally. I tend to think that shit happens to everybody and I try and just put it behind me. I can't change the past, but I can do something about the future so I may as well get on with it. That's the way I look at it.

DIEDERIK: I think there's a lot of hard work involved in your success! If you were helping someone else, a young veterinarian, what pitfalls would tell them to make sure that they avoid?

VERA: Every human is different in the way their brain works and what makes them happy, and they need to go with what is right for them morally and physically, and not be pushed into someone else's bunch of beliefs. And, I see that happen in veterinary practices; I think it probably happens in every walk of life, but in veterinary practices, which are very dictatorial or very personality driven or whatever, where the members of the practice can't be themselves, the practice doesn't really meld with who they are, they should leave the practice and find a place where they are happy.

DIEDERIK: What is your passion in practice?

VERA: Life is my passion

My passion in practice was surgery, and I loved it. I love surgery, and in particular, orthopaedic surgery. I love just getting it done and then, *"Hey, you've got a result."* It's super.

DIEDERIK: You've obviously differentiated the business side of practice from the clinical side. When did you start to look at those two as separate entities?

VERA: After my first year out. I have always been involved with various business ideas through my family. So, that probably helped me to think that, *"Hey, you can give things ago, and it's amazing what can happen."* I had one piece of advice from my grandfather, which was there's got to be more money coming in than going out, therefore it's easy to run a business.

I can't say that I truly separated it. If a practice is clinically running well, the money sort of naturally follows as long as everyone is honest, fair and works hard. And as I would say to a client, *"I want to eat too, and I think that my staff deserve a good wage for a good day's work."*

I think the business side was sort of just part of me from the very start because I'd been involved in all sorts of other businesses, and still am.

DIEDERIK: Our industry has a bit of a 'reputation'. What do you think kept you sane?

VERA: Work. The only times I felt down is when personal things where bad, and work was my saviour. And when clients where occasionally difficult, as they are sometimes, I just put that down to some people being a pain or just generally miserable people, and that's not my problem.

DIEDERIK: What's the biggest thing or things that you or your practice have given back to your community?

VERA: Listening and supporting so many members of the community, especially the old, the infirm or the lonely, and the time we can spend with them and going the extra mile. If you're a local vet, it gives you insights into people's lives. I had people come in to the surgery, put their dog on the floor, and they'd tell me all their problems. And then they'd say, *"There's actually nothing the matter with the dog Vera, but I needed to talk to somebody."* And I'd go, *"So this is one of these. Can I still charge you $60?"*

I spend a lot of time, even now, going to visit people who can't get in. I'm doing a lot of house-calls and chatting to people who can't visit us. Because I've known three generations of families now. So, I would know their situation, and one can be empathetic or sympathetic, or whatever, to their situation, and they just want somebody who can listen, because everybody else is so time poor.

DIEDERIK: I wholeheartedly agree. I think one of the biggest joys in practices is developing relationships over the long term and having good, almost friends – if you like – coming in to see you.

VERA: And that is totally what happens. Absolutely I agree with that, to the point when now—and I'm only working one day a week now—that I have a whole bunch of people that I see regularly and visit their homes because they can't get up. And a bunch of people that I take to the theatre every two months, another bunch of people that I take out to pizza once a month, and there are all sorts of clients that have been long-term friends, but then it became people who don't have big community links, and this kind of keeps them in the loop.

DIEDERIK: What are, three drivers or attributes to success?

VERA: Be confident enough to take some risks. You won't succeed if you don't try. And, do your best.

DIEDERIK: What's your vision for the future of the veterinary industry?

VERA: Humans are just another mammal; is the way I look at it. We as vets, are uniquely placed to have a balanced view of the animal environmental interaction, and I think we can contribute enormously to helping the understanding of the natural world, and our place in it as humans, and the importance of the interaction of living things in the environment that makes us all content. The veterinary profession is an important cog in conveying these messages on many levels.

I think vets can play an important part in the whole one-health one-earth idea.

DIEDERIK: Was there ever a turning point, a snap point, a line in the sand or a defining moment in your life or in your career? And if so, when was it, and what was it?

VERA: That's really easy because I don't think there ever was one. I see life as a continuum. A slow getting of wisdom.

DIEDERIK: Vera, thank you very much for your answers. They've been insightful. I appreciate the time you've spent with me today.

Key Take-Aways

- It's important to listen and observe – both the pets you're working with and their owners
- Be bold and try new procedures or treatment. Keep educated and read worldly, even outside of veterinary science
- Success; feeling like I've done some good at the end of the day
- *"It uses less facial muscles, and therefore, you'll get less wrinkles if you smile, rather than frown."*
- Not taking opportunities is the biggest mistake you can make, because there are opportunities everywhere and you've just got to grab them with both hands and run with them

> **"Most veterinarians graduate with a double major. A major in Veterinary Science and a second major in Procrastination. For God's sake – just take action."**
>
> Diederik Gelderman

Author's Final Word

You've read the stories, you've heard the wisdom and now it's your turn…

Remember that the key to making a change in your life, in your career or in your business is YOU! That's right, the buck stops there. If you think you can do it, then you are right, and if you think you can't, then you are also right.

You too can achieve what these practitioners have achieved. Having practice and financial success, having a successful career and creating a worthwhile life are all well within your reach.

It's not rocket science, you don't have to be extraordinarily gifted as a veterinarian, as a marketer or as a business person.

You just need to decide which road you are going to travel, the type of practice and lifestyle that you want to have and then get cracking and stick to your guns, keep at it and keep plugging away. You may not know it now, but you will reach your goals far more quickly than you might have thought.

As I was doing these interviews, there is one thing that just kept on jumping out at me in interview after interview…. and it's this – **you can't do it alone**.

To get where you want to go and get there quickly, you need help, support and guidance. You need friends, family and colleagues and then you need a guide or a mentor. Someone who's been there, who's helped others get there; someone who can show you the shortcuts, help you around the obstacles and how to avoid the quicksand.

This person will take years off your journey as well as saving you a huge amount of stress, angst, ennui, backtracking and financial cost.

My advice to you is that you immediately find yourself such a person and get yourself mentored. Whether that be formally or informally doesn't matter – just do it.

One word of caution – ensure that they've been there and 'done it' themselves and that they've also helped others. They must have walked the talk.

If you're not sure where to find such a person, then give me a holler. You can ring me on 0408 793 337 or you can email me on <u>diederikgelderman@ gmail.com</u>

I'll help you find a mentor who is the right fit and match for you.

Lastly, here are two phrases that I love:
- Success leaves clues
- Good veterinary business is simple

The BIGGEST mistakes I see in modern 'vet' are these:
- Aspiring practitioners who do not copy, mimic or ethically plagiarise from those who are successful. In fact, most aspiring practitioners rarely ask for help, rarely model successful practitioners and seem determined to 'go it alone' and/or to 'recreate the wheel'.
- Veterinarians seem determined to make business success complicated, when exactly the opposite strategy is what works best. Veterinary business is simple and when you keep it simple, you'll be successful and you'll have a successful practice.

So be your own best friend, best mentor, best champion and best ally in your veterinary career. Take everything you've learned and make the change that you know you deserve – do it TODAY.

Let me close by saying:

- 🐾 My passion is for pets and people and our fantastic industry and I'm here for you.

- 🐾 My purpose is to help you improve and grow your veterinary career and/or your veterinary business by helping you implement proven, powerful, practical and simple to apply strategies, techniques, tools and tips which will give you immediate results.

> **I'm here to be of assistance to you in ANY way at all – even just as someone to bounce some ideas off, just reach out and make contact – I'd be chuffed and super-delighted to help.**

About the Author

Dr Diederik Gelderman

Author, Veterinarian & Veterinary Business Coach

Diederik is an author, an award-winning veterinarian, and a much sought after veterinary business coach.

Being drawn to horses at an early age, Diederik participated in equestrian competition from the age of five through to his second year of University, when he devoted all of his attention to completing veterinary school.

Upon graduation from veterinary school he purchased a small, one-person clinic. He rapidly grew the clinic into a business with four locations, eight veterinarians, and a large support staff. In 2004, the practice won the Pfizer/AVA Practice of Excellence Award and came 3rd in the Fujitsu Customer Service Awards.

Diederik began coaching veterinary professionals with his Turbo Charge Your Veterinary Practice seminars in 2004. By 2009, his seminars expanded internationally to Hong Kong, New Zealand, Europe, South Africa and the United States. That same year, he sold his practice, allowing him to concentrate full-time on his passion for helping veterinary practices achieve business excellence. However, the call of clinical practice is still so great that Diederik still spends one day every week doing clinical work.

Since establishing his worldwide reputation as a coach to veterinarians wanting to improve their profitability, he has coached or consulted with more than 350 small to medium-sized enterprises in a diverse range of industries.

Diederik's professional associations include the Australian Veterinary Business Association of which he was president in 2015 and 2016. He is also a member of the Australian Veterinary Association Practice Management group, Vet Partners, the Australian Veterinary Association, the American Association of Equine Practitioners, the Australian Association of Practice Management, the Australian Association of Veterinary Diagnostic Imaging, the American Animal Hospital Association, and the American Veterinary Medical Association.

In his spare time, Diederik enjoys scuba diving, playing chess, reading, horse riding, and competing in squash. He also speaks Dutch, French, German, Spanish, and Italian.

He has travelled and worked throughout France, Germany, Italy, Switzerland, USA, Spain, Fiji, Japan, New Zealand, Thailand, South Africa, Hong Kong, and many of the Pacific Islands.

Diederik Gelderman is the author of *Veterinary Success Secrets Revealed* and lives in the beautiful Southern Highlands of New South Wales, Australia with his lovely partner Jennifer, his horses, donkey, dogs, cats, birds, alpacas and pet cows.

Recommended Resources

Imagine What You Could Accomplish Working With Your Own Personal Business Coach ...

I have been consulting, coaching and mentoring in the veterinary and business world and studying human potential for over two decades and one thing has become very clear to me over time...

After working with thousands of individuals, excellent practices and stand-out companies, I find that most already know exactly what they need to do to create outrageous results in every area of their practice and their life...they just don't do it!

The fact is...high achievers (in any field) who have consultants, coaches or mentors always achieve more than those who don't. This is well documented, I've seen this time and again, and I've experienced it myself.

Just think about it, anyone at the top of their game; whether that's in business, finance, leadership, management, martial arts or professional sports, and the results will be the same – they've all had valuable guidance and direction, and more often than not, it comes in the form of a mentor, consultant or coach.

So, if you're Serious About Taking Your Life or Business to the Next Level...

Talk to Diederik about his One of One Consulting Services. You can contact him via;

diederikgelderman@gmail.com
(M) +61 (0)408 793337
(M) +61 (0)2 48834938

> I'll consult with you one-on-one to make all of your business goals a reality in your veterinary practice.
>
> *Diederik Gelderman*

Rich Vet, Poor Vet

This is a special offer from Chris Newton, author of this remarkable little book.

Simply email Chris at chris@ultimateveterinarypractice.com and mention that you'd like a free PDF version of his complete book ... and he'll send it to you with his compliments. No strings attached. (The hard copy sells for AUD$24.95.)

Why you should send for Chris Newton's Rich Vet, Poor Vet today...

In the words of the author: "In recent years, I've spoken with scores of veterinarian practice owners in Australia and the UK. I haven't met many who say they want to be rich. I haven't heard even one say that. But I haven't met one who said they wanted to be POOR either.

"Rich Vet, Poor Vet takes you on an eye-opening journey, first to identify the stumbling blocks that may be holding you back in achieving joy and 'richness of life' from your practice. And then, strap yourself in as you head into the future, where your practice runs like clockwork, with a happy and energised team of people, clients who rave about you, and a whole new potential for growth and increased profitability, whether you're there, or sitting on a beach somewhere, a million miles from a phone."

Take Chris up on his special free, no strings attached offer now. Simply email him at chris@ultimateveterinarypractice.com and mention that you'd like to receive a free PDF version of his complete book ... and he'll send it to you with his compliments.

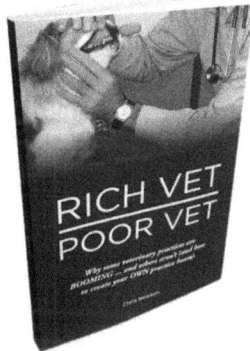

Getting the Right Finance for Your Practice

When you need finance to grow your practice, when you need to lease or rent equipment, cars and the like, when getting finance for that investment property or holiday house, it's not as easy as it used to be.

The days of walking into your local branch, 'tipping your hat' for a loan approval are well gone.

In fact, if your Branch Manager, or loan representative doesn't have a relationship with the decision maker (credit assessor) the likelihood of your loan being approved is very low.

What's more, many of the commercial lenders see veterinarians as an 'easy touch' and they may be prepared to loan them money, but the conditions and rates are poorer than they could be.

Vets are experts in looking after pets and other animals, they are not experts in money and finance. So, when you need finance for your practice or even personally, you need to work with someone who is an expert in the field of veterinary finance.

Let me introduce Paul Lloyd from Stimulus Finance. He's your go-to-guy for all your financial needs.

Paul Lloyd Dip FS (FMBM)
49 Porter St, Prahran VIC 3181
P: (03) 9525 2025 I F: (03) 9525 2026
M: 0411 277 336 I E: paul@stimulusfinance.com.au
W: www.stimulusfinance.com.au

STIMULUS | FINANCE

You Need to Join a Supportive Online Community

Make Your Next Conference or Meeting a Success With a Dynamic Speaker/Trainer

Whether you need to motivate your team, increase sales, boost income, increase performance, expand creativity, improve leadership, enhance communication, find more balance, reduce stress or improve client and customer service – these disciplines, when put into practice, will create massive and permanent change in the lives of your participants and in the day-to-day operation and functioning of your practice.

PRESENTATION FORMATS

Keynote

This engaging, thought-provoking program will leave your conference or meeting participants energised and excited about the material they have just learned.

Please allow 1 to 2 hours.

Full Day or Half Workshops

This is a 4 to 8 hour tailored program to suit your and your practice's outcomes and objectives. This is a 'workshop' and therefore utilises exercises, activities and group experiences, rather than simple lecture, to achieve awareness and personal growth among participants. Includes key learning tools and handouts.

Please allow 4 to 8 hours.

2- or 3-Day Corporate Training

Perfect for high performance teams, team leaders or managers where participants will encounter peak performance or staff management issues on an ongoing basis. We help your people find their own personal 'Blackbelt' in peak performance so they can apply it to their daily work environment, helping them to grow and expand their thinking, leadership abilities and comfort zones.

So, if you're Serious About Making Your Next Meeting or Conference a Winner...

Talk to Diederik about his One on One Consulting Services. You can contact him via;

diederikgelderman@gmail.com

(M) +61 (0)408 793337

(M) +61 (0)2 48834938

Veterinary Practice Management Software

Would you prefer to be only paying $1,350 AUS* per clinic per year for your Practice Management System without losing any functionality?

- Regardless of how many workstations?
- No extra fees for connection to peripherals?
- No extra fees for setting up additional workstations or laptops?
- No extra fees for setting up SMS or email reminders?
- Unlimited support included?
- No on-going licence fees?
- All upgrades and updates included?
- Access your system anytime from anywhere (with internet connection)?
- No limit to database size?

This is easily done by changing over to Clinic-Ware!

Clinic-Ware is a mature system that has been available for 10 years. Clinic-Ware is installed on your own server so it is secure and you can still work if there is an internet failure. All support is done online and we pride ourselves in getting back to our clients within hours, not days.

There is an initial one-off fee of $5,800 AUS* (The only other fee is $1,000 AUS* for full data audit and conversion) which covers:

- Lifetime licence fee (transferrable if you sell your clinic).
- All installation, connection, setting up of printers etc. regardless of how many workstations.
- Full training.
- First year's (unlimited) support.

I would like to show you how easy our system is to use with an online demonstration. It quite literally will take 30 minutes of your time.

Another huge factor is simplicity of use. When you purchase Clinic-Ware, you will receive all the training you need, within the initial licence fee, to get you up & running – no extra cost.

Clinic-Ware – It WORKS !!!

*All prices current at 2017-18 and will be held until Christmas 2018 to new users on production of this advert. These prices are RESERVED for readers of this book only. When you contact Clinic-Ware – say that Dr Diederik Gelderman sent you (to receive this offer).

"Would I recommend the Ultimate Veterinary Practice program to other vets?…"

As a result of the UVP program, we started growing fairly fast. To be honest, faster than I anticipated. For a short time, it actually created a cash-flow issue for us. It was a great problem to have because it made us more systemised in our financial management too. A double bonus. Would I recommend it to other vets? Well, let me put it to you this way. Just get your credit card out and go for it. The program works!

– Mike Woodham, Sugarland Vet Clinic

"Six months in, we were financially able and confident in the team to take a 7 week holiday with the kids …"

Focusing on customer service in the 'moments of truth' module has taken away the need to discount, and we're getting lots of new clients every week from referrals. The consulting room process has been pure gold…we no longer have missed charges and we no longer have to talk about money. The way the program enabled us to educate the team means they've taken over that function and they love it, because they believe in it…

One of the first systems we put into action was the Dental System. Everything is pre-done, so we just had to implement it. We went from doing four or five dentals a month to now, 20 to 25, and I reckon we can double that… Six months into the program, we were financially able and confident in the team to be able to take a long overdue holiday…seven weeks of caravanning with the kids…we heard from the team only once. Previously I would have thought that was unachievable. But now we've got another seven-week holiday planned for this year. And we're still growing month on month.

– Michael Bassett, Montrose Veterinary Clinic

"Up to 188% increase in response to vaccine reminders."

We are loving the Ultimate Veterinary Practice program. By using just one small part of the program, we got up to 188% increase in our response rates to vaccine reminders. It really is done-for-you marketing that works. With a huge impact on our bottom line.

– David Stasiuk, Cheltenham Vet Clinic, Victoria

"I was a bit sceptical at first."

We run a four-vet practice in a somewhat economically challenged area, so I was concerned about the return on investment. But after the lag effect all the marketing concepts started working their magic. I actually had to double check the figures. I couldn't believe we were turning over so much.

We're up by in excess of $100,000 for the first six months of this year, and the really great thing is the staff are implementing the program for us. It took a little bit of setting up at first, but now it is just part of our system. A great business investment.

– Michael Featherstone, Blue and White Vet Clinic

"Another 30 booked in so far next week …"

We launched our Seniors' Program based on the Ultimate Veterinary Practice program last week and the results have been fantastic, generating over $2,000 in the first week and a very good uptake of return visits for dentals, etc. In our first week, we undertook 30+ complimentary Seniors Checks, with another 30 booked in so far next week. Plus return visit bookings in coming weeks.

– Taryn Baker, Practice Admin, Clare Valley Veterinary Services

With comments like this from vet practices using the Ultimate Veterinary Practice 'secret weapon' …

Maybe it really is something 'out of the box'!

You'll never know until you get all the facts for yourself. Ask for a no obligation information pack.

Email: **enquiries@ultimateveterinarypractice.com**
Or ring 07 33006909 or 0408 793337

THE
ULTIMATE
VETERINARY PRACTICE

PET PACK

Starting when James was a practising veterinarian using simple call back tools, Pet Pack has grown into a business that services the full range of veterinary clinic online marketing requirements, including:

Websites - it's important to have a website that looks good and performs. Pet Pack designs are tailored to the vet's requirements while maintaining and measuring high performance. Installing a premium performance site will generate twice the calls of the average vet clinic website within 12-18 months.

Pet Pack expertise extends to:
· Google AdWords
· Google My Business
· Content
· SEO, and
· Call tracking

Email Newsletters - keeping in touch with clients is the key to effective pet care relationships. Pet Pack provides a high grade service that allows clinics to get a personalised communication out on time every month, improving treatment compliance and bringing clients back to the clinic more often.

Facebook - Pet Pack exists to help clinics make their page an effective way to engage with their community. Working closely with the clinic, this service supports vets to grow their pages beyond 1000 Likes.

Online Performance Assessment - if you're wondering how you're performing online, get an expert analysis of your online presence from Pet Pack. This assessment is a great way to start improving your online performance, as it will give you the information needed to make informed decisions about your online presence.

(03) 9690 6253   info@petpack.com.au

Give Your New Grads a Great Head-Start

Your 'Face' on the Phone is Critical to Your Success